Surviving the Holocaust

True Stories Of Auschwitz Survivors & War Crimes Of The Second World War

Margalit Kafni

Korman's Prayer

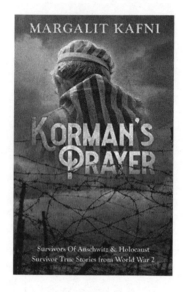

To live through the atrocities of World War II and the worst work camp in history, will no doubt change a person.

It shows how despite the worst circumstances, people can still show love and compassion toward one another. It strives to show that no matter how cruel the torture, the one thing the enemy cannot take is our spirit.

This novel is inspired by the story of Henry Korman's life. It will give you an in-depth look at what life was like inside the barbed-wire fences of Auschwitz. It will also show you the effect that these experiences had on one man, leading him away from anger and hate, toward a life of service to others. A few years before he died, Henry was quoted as saying: "I worry what will happen when I and others like me are no longer here to tell the story. I want people to keep reading about it and for them to leave tears on the paper."

I hope that this book does exactly that.

Margalit Kafni

READ NOW ON AMAZON

Table of Contents

Please observe a minute of silence for all that was lost during the Holocaust

May G-d bless us all

Shalom

Description

The world suddenly changed into hell as the rivers and lakes turned into blood. The Pacific Ocean and the Atlantic Ocean could not be left behind. The hue and cries of people could be heard from afar and beyond, as the merciless and ruthless massacre of the Jews were being carried out. This was the genocide that took place between 1941 and 1945.

This book, *Surviving the Holocaust*, opens up a fresh wound that, even though we are healed, the wound looks fresh just like yesterday. The book talks much about the survivors of the Holocaust. The main objective of this book is to instill in you the information and the facts in order for you to understand what went on during that time.

This book explores the life of the survivors and how they managed their ordeals. It is good to note that the likes of Irene Fogel saw death with their own eyes. Imagine existing in an era where over 60 million people are being displaced, with another 17 million that just disappeared. It is painful, indeed. Irene, who survived the Holocaust, was born in a poverty-stricken family, even though her father's lumber yard was able to sustain them. It is now up to you to check on this chapter so that you can gather more information about Irene and the other survivors.

This book also elaborates and illustrates why this war started. Some put these reasons as mere conceptions, while others believe in them. The life of the survivors even became hell after the Holocaust, since keeping up with the situation proved horrific. Many went ahead to commit suicide.

This book, *Surviving the Holocaust*, is an emotional book. It is filled with detailed content that you might require in your quest for knowing World War II. I cannot dwell on all the chapters here, but within the book, you will learn about the following:

- Reasons that the Holocaust cannot fade

- The effects of World War II
- The misconceptions about the Holocaust

And so much more.

Introduction

In 1941, the world became dull, and many across the European countries were intoxicated into a somber mood. The atmosphere was humid and smelled like nothing but fresh blood. The rivers turned red as they deposited their blood water into the lakes and oceans. And this was the story of the genocide that took place between 1941 and 1945. The Holocaust genocide, which is also called the "Shoah", was a massacre that was being used to eliminate the European Jews. During the first time, around six million Jews lost their lives. Mass shootings and other modes of killing were the order of the day.

Another method that was used was by extermination, killing in gas chambers, and gas vans. However, the genocide war could not use other means of killing other than ethnic cleansing. It should be noted that, during this time, over 11 million people got persecuted. Many studies are looking for the real motives of why the genocide took place. However, most of them come up with the issue of anti-Semitism. It is also good to note that, during this era, over sixty million people couldn't find homes. They were displaced totally. Some were poisoned and later killed, while others were made slaves forever. Even though many people were later prosecuted, the scar will never fade. The Jew community faced a near-impossible situation in the German-occupied territories. Their attempt to stage a severe revolt was thwarted by a lack of access to arms.

Furthermore, the Jews were often surrounded by the native anti-Semitic population. The other part of the population was restrained from putting their lives on the line to help the Jews. In other terms, the Jewish community found itself against a whole German community. Under Weimar's reign, the laws passed over the prohibitions on homosexuality. However, the lenience ended in 1933 when the Nazis violently attacked gay bars. The Nazis made homosexual intent an unbiased reason for prosecution. Male homosexuals were detained and confined in the concentration camps (no systematic persecution of lesbians was recorded). The detained gays wore yellow armbands.

Overview

Following the collapse of the Nazi government, the Nazi leadership tried several ways to get rid of the evidence and even run away from justice. The allied forces established an International Military Tribunal (IMT) in Nuremberg. The tribunal was made up of two representatives from each of the four allies. The aim of the tribunal was mainly to put to trail the captured high-ranking Nazis.

In total, 24 high-ranking Nazi leaders were arraigned before the IMT. The charges brought against the accused ranged from: Crimes against humanity, war crimes, crimes against peace, and conspiracy. Of the 24, 13 were found guilty, and were sentenced to death—seven of the accused got sentences ranging from 10 years to life in prison. Three others were acquitted, while one committed suicide while awaiting trial.

The IMT also found out that those three organizations that were used by the Nazis as government machinery tools were nothing more than criminal organizations. They were: Gestapo-SD, the Leadership Corps of the Nazi Party, and the SS. Historians have had multiple debates over the origin of the Holocaust, hence coming up with two explanatory blocks: The initialism and the functionalism. Both of the two historical bodies tried to explain the cause, plan, and Hitler's strategic approach to getting rid of the Jews.The initialisms believe that the Nazi leader, Adolph Hitler, had already planned the extermination of the Jewish from as early as 1918 (during World War I). Adolph Hitler presumed that the Germans were a special and superior race, so he planned and oversaw the execution of the event. The functionalisms, on the other hand, claim that the plans of the vast extermination were built up and had evolved in bits as a result of multiple responses from bureaucrats who were responding to some of their other policy failures. The debate still goes on up-to-date, but I think that both ideologies by historians have equal merit, and have settled to a large degree. Nazism entailed projection and implementations by the Nazis, and all subjects were expected to adhere without demure.

Many people still try to figure out why the Nazis were out to get some specific persons, for instance, the Jews. For the longest time possible, the Jews have undergone vast rejection from other racial existence. A large sum of factors has contributed to the environment under which atrocities have been committed all over the world, specifically targeting some identities. The Jews had faced general racism from other races for some time before the Holocaust. They were considered more or less superior (or, rather, inferior) when compared to the rest. This made them very vulnerable to the threat coming from the "more superior" races.

Part I: The Historical Context

Chapter 1: The History of the Second World War

It has been argued that that the First World War set the stage for the second by creating instability in Europe. The Second World War proved to be the most disheartening conflict in history. The rise of Adolf Hitler in Germany stirred the war on many fronts. Hitler rose to power at a time when the economy and politics of Germany were not steady. Together with his Nazi party, Hitler signed deliberate pacts with Italy and Japan, intending to dominate the world, thereby proving the superiority of the German peoples. The assault on Poland, a territory that the allies had sworn to protect, in September 1939, invited the French and British to declare war on Germany, marking the beginning of the Second World War. The war would end up claiming more lives, destroying more land and properties, and leaving many lasting impacts on the lives of the victims and the generations to follow. The war that lasted six years became the most destructive in the history of global conflicts. The estimated number of people killed in battle ranged from sixty to eighty million. Amongst the casualties, a whopping six million Jews died in the Nazi concentration camps as part of Hitler's diabolical "Final Solution," now known as the Holocaust.

The following present the key events during the Second World War:

The Clash Near the Marco Polo Bridge (7 July 1937)

The beginning of the full-on clash between Japan and China was initiated by an incomprehensible battle between Japanese units on a military exercise near the Marco Polo Bridge, southwest of Beijing. The Japanese felt their honor had been challenged and questioned, thereby sending a delegation of troops to the region. Despots in the Japanese army took advantage of the incident to ask for China as a settlement in their favor. However, the Chinese pro-independence leader, Jiang Jieshi, refused to bow down to the demands of the Japanese. In the end, an obstinate brawl broke out, weakening the Japanese and the Chinese altogether. Toward the end of July, a large-scale conflict broke out, leading to the assault and occupation of Beijing by the Japanese.

Germans' Offensives to the West (10 May 1940)

The Hitler-led Germany refused to limit their assault after the invasion of Poland. Hitler's failure to engage in evocative negotiations and pacts also led to the spread of the war to other parts of the world. The successful conquest of Poland offered Germany an advantage to fight the war on one front. The opportunity motivated Hitler to urge his troops to march west, stating that Germany was more prepared for the war as compared to either France or Britain. Hitler had to suspend the attacks until 1 May 1940. The delay was due to adverse weather conditions in Germany around 1940.

Besides, there were several warnings from the high commander of Germany based on the need for adequate preparation, which delayed the assaults. The invasion of France followed the charges. The surprise attack proved effective since Britain and France failed to rally a fluid defense mechanism. The following seven weeks saw Germany marshal a campaign to transform the situation in Europe by acquiring vast territories. The triumph strengthened Hitler's belief in his unavoidable success.

A Look at the Battle of Britain

The fall of France made it easy for Germany to invade near the territory of Britain, and on 12 August 1940, the first intensive assault on the airfields of Britain was hurled. Hitler commanded the German air force to drive the British warships from the channel and clear the way for more charges to follow. However, the *Luftwaffe* (air force) commanders got progressively more worried about launching an assault on the RAF and its secondary structures to pave the way for the imminent assault. Instead, the air force tried to force Britain into submission by a bombing war on civilian targets—a line of attack that would put the air force on the center stage.

The battle of Britain, the most massive military war in history to be fought in the air, saw the German air force launch a series of attacks on Britain's air defense forces. However, the RAF emerged victorious in the war by the end of October 1940. The German troops failed to coordinate their air attack and the cropping land invasion units, leading to their defeat in the Battle of Britain. Additionally, the Germans lacked strategic air offense units. On the other hand, the British proved to possess good radar and ground control coordination—a critical element that led to their triumph in the war.

Operation Barbarossa (22 June 1941)

With victories over Poland, Belgium, and the Netherlands, Hitler grew overconfident. He developed a disdain for other political systems, and wanted to destroy their governments to obtain the living space he so dearly craved. The urge to invade the Soviet Union grew. Hitler grew more concerned about the intentions of Stalin, concluding that a war with the communists was unavoidable. These delusions gave Hitler more confidence that an assault on the Soviet Union would be straightforward. He thus received a host of misleading military intelligence and assessments of the size of the red army and their potential to mobilize their troops. Hitler had the belief that a defeat of the Soviet Union would make Britain submit to Germany's dominance of Europe. The confidence led Hitler into launching the operation 'Barbarossa', his worst mistake in the history of the warfare. On 22 June, the German troops launched a surprise attack on the Soviet Union. The attacks lacked any systematic plan. In the end, Germany found itself dragging in on a war that would lead to its eventual defeat.

The Attack on Pearl Harbor (7 December 1941)

In what was seen as a clear act of war, the Japanese attacked the base of the American Pacific Fleet at Pearl Harbor on the island of Oahu in the Hawaiian archipelago. The Japanese saw the attack as a warning to the United States to stop opposing the expansion strategy of Japan. The Japanese strategized to wreck the entire American Pacific Fleet. The plan could be viewed as a conscious operational success on one side, and a tactical disaster on the other.

The damage done to the American battleships at Pearl Harbor forced the Americans to put more emphasis on better naval planning. The Americans would put more emphasis on the three ships that were not present at the time of the attack (the Lexington, the Yorktown, and the Enterprise). Due to the emphasis on destroying the battleships, not the equipment and installation, the attack on Pearl Harbor remained the most significant attack on any fleet in the history of the war.

In the course of the war, the flaws in the strategic concepts that underpinned the Japanese plans were unearthed. First, the Japanese had underrated the financial might of the United States and the resolve of the people. Secondly, the Japanese went too far to launch an assault that was not necessary.

However, the massive sizes of the Japanese battleship, especially in carriers and cruisers, could not compare to the American fleets at Pearl Harbor. The attack on Pearl Harbor marked the official entry of the U.S. in the Second World War.

Battle of Midway (4 June 1942)

The might of the American navy was experienced in the battle of midway, where the Americans triumphed. The struggle also mirrored the strength of the American intelligence and repair efforts, having come from an attack (by the Japanese). The coordination of the American carriers and bombers proved crucial in the battle.

While the Americans grew more organized in handling uncertainties, the Japanese remained undecided on the tactics to employ. The Japanese faced the dilemma of deciding whether to prepare their aircraft for land or ship targets—a point of concern that delayed the battle.

The capability of the Americans to learn from the previous battle of the Coral Sea and the reliance on their strategic skillfulness was extremely substantial in the struggle. The Americans relied on the two to locate Japanese targets. The Japanese found themselves unable to respond to the attacks by the American dive-bombers—which was a trivial example of failed coordination.

The attacks shifted the numbers of the carrier power in the pacific. In no time, the Japanese found themselves short of well-trained aggressive soldiers in the waters. It proved challenging to replace the lost pilots, not least due to the shortage of fuel for the drills. The loss of four carriers' maintenance crews dealt a considerable blow to the efforts of the Japanese to win the battle.

The Japanese lost all of their four heavy carriers, leading to the triumph of the United States in the battle. In the end, the American carrier strategy manifested itself as a 'lack-of-battleship' strategy.

Battle of Kursk (5 July 1943)

The contest is considered the last major attack launched by the Germans on the Eastern Front. The Germans opted to capitalize on the opportunities provided by the critical German salient. Hitler took to tactical hopeful discernment, viewing the battle as a total extinction that he could prevail in (he considered himself superior). Hitler knew that victory in this attack would demoralize the allies by dwindling their confidence in the possibility of any Soviet success. However, the Germans found themselves outnumbered, owing to the preparedness of the Soviet defense mechanism that frustrated all German offenses. The Germans suffered vast loses, forcing Hitler to call off the attacks. The withdrawal of German forces allowed the Soviets to counterstrike, driving the Germans back.

The D-Day (6 June 1944)

The D-Day, the landing of the Allied Forces in northern France, commenced on 6 June 1944. On that day, the American, British, and Canadian forces landed in Normandy. The Allied troops had strategized the landing (referred to as operation 'Neptune') and the invasion of the region (termed operation 'Overload'). The operations were a success, owing to the well-organized and in-effect naval support for the air assault. Additionally, the Allied succeeded in their deception exercise, operation 'Fortitude', taking the Normandy by surprise.

All this happened due to the Germans' concentration on their defenses and troops in the Calais region. The Calais region presented a small sea crossing and a shorter route to Germany. On the other hand, the Normandy was easily accessible through the assault ports on the south coast of England (particularly the ports of Plymouth, Portland, and Portsmouth). Additionally, the Germans lacked adequate naval firepower and human resources to stop the annexation.

The German commanders were often at loggerheads concerning the right course of action to take. On many occasions, they failed to agree on a suitable way to retaliate. Most surprisingly, the commanders were split on crucial decisions. A section wanted to move German ten panzer divisions close to the coast to attack the allies before they could consolidate positions. Another camp tried to keep them as strategic reserves for the war. The failure to have one decision-making mechanism resulted in a rift within the German ranks.

The landing took different forms. For instance, the British designed individual tanks to attack the coastal defenses, in particular, the Crab-wave vessels to attack the minefields in Gold, Juno, and Sword beaches. The strategy worked well. The Allied forces (Canadians and British) that landed on the shore seized cover-positions as a strategic plan for the combat against the German troops.

Contrary to their Canadian and British counterparts, the American forces that landed on the Omaha beach fell short of a good war strategy. Their misery began with the misguided assault, the Duplex drive, which landed way far off the shores. The American troops also failed to use the specialized arsenal in the attack. The aftermath saw the Americans sustaining massive casualties from the unsuccessful landing and the positions of the cliffs that had not been well-crushed by the airstrikes.

However, the Americans managed to jump the huddle and march inward. At the end of D-Day, the jumping-off point was not deep enough, exposing the troops to the danger of German assault. The Americans were, nevertheless, lucky that the Germans lacked enough armor to stage a response. The failure of the Germans to mount a response mirrored the inelasticity stemming from Hitler's interference.

Operation 'Overload' marked a significant advancement in the assaults by sea and land, as the need to capture a port to land, reinforce, and support the invasion force was not necessary.

The allies never intended to seize the ports, much to the disappointment of the Germans who had conflicting anticipations. The structured design of the assault worked to the benefit of the allies. They laid oil pipelines under the channel to help maintain supplies.

However, the tactics employed in the invasions proved difficult for the Allied forces to break out of the Normandy (although they prospered in August).

Battle of Leyte Gulf (23–26 October 1944)

In mid-October 1944, the United States took advantage of its mighty and growing naval and air forces to launch an attack to recapture the Philippines. The operation led to the beginning of the Battle of Leyte

Gulf—the most massive maritime battle of the Second World War. The U.S. used the fight to secure naval preeminence in the Western Pacific.

The operations of the American forces in the Philippines presented a lot of challenges to the Japanese. Aware of their imminent defeat, Japanese naval leaders objected to losing honorably. On 18 October 1944, the leader of the Naval Operations Section requested that the Japanese fleets be recognized as "a fitting place to die" and accorded "the chance to bloom as flowers of death."

The Japanese deployed their fleets as bait in an attempt to lure the American carriers off the shore of the Philippines in an operation dubbed as 'Sho-Go' (the action of the victor). They then use two striking naval forces to attack the vulnerable landing American fleet. The intricate scheming by the Japanese proved challenging to read and handle appropriately by the American commanders.

The Japanese nearly offered tangible resistance when they approached the allies' landing zone. The Japanese strike force was far more superior to the Americans, but failed to attack. The strike force backed off due to a lack of adequate naval skills to read the locations of the enemy warships. The inexperience resulted in the defeat of the Japanese in the hands of the Americans. The American forces destroyed four Japanese carriers, three battleships (including the Musashi), ten cruisers, other warships, and aircraft.

The Second Atomic Bomb Dropped on Japan (9 August 1945)

The second atomic bomb dropped on Nagasaki by the United States was more effective compared to the first one on Hiroshima. The attack indicated that America was ready to mount unstoppable bombing processes. The bombing reduced an area close to seven kilometer square to ashes. The attack killed more than seventy-three thousand people, maiming more than seventy-four thousand, and leaving long-lasting health consequences.

As a result, Japan was forced to surrender unconditionally. On 15th August 1945, an imperial broadcast announced the halt of the aggressions following Emperor Hirohito's involvement at the Imperial Conference on 9 and 14 August.

Chapter 2: The Holocaust

The word "Holocaust," derived from the Greek phrase "holokaustos" (whole burnt sacrifice), was historically used to refer to a burned offering. In Hebrew, the term meant far more than that. Other parts denoted it as "catastrophe" or "destruction." However, ever since the Great War, the term had been used to mean the massacre of more than six million Jewish people, including women and children, by the Nazis. The Nazis termed the killings as "the final solution" to the Jewish problem. Led by Adolf Hitler, the anti-Semitic Nazis perceived the Jews as a weak race, and which posed a threat to the German ethnic wholesomeness and society as a whole. The mass prosecution of the Jews as part of Hitler's final solution strategy, executed in concentration camps in Poland, is the present-day Holocaust.

Throughout history, artists have come up with phrases to describe the Holocaust. Raul Hilberg referred to the Holocaust as "the destruction of Jews of European origin," while Lucy S. Dawidowicz termed it as "the war against the Jews." Other artists have shown in their works, both in literature and film, how the Nazis used World War II to wage ethnic hostilities against the Jews. The term "Holocaust" has been used in history to refer to the mass killing of the Jews. The use follows definitive demonstration of the massacre in selected extermination camps, where the bodies of the victims were burned in open fire.

Long before the Nazis rose to power in 1933, they had already let their hatred toward the Jews become known. By 1919, Adolf Hitler had written a memoir, entitled *Mein Kampf (My Struggle)*, a controversial book that openly supported his anti-Semitic ideology. The book's objective was to encourage the Nazis to "clear" all the Jews and create space for the pure Germans. *My Struggle* also portrayed the Jews as a "weak race" who were supposed to be exterminated. In the first volume, Hitler posited that the annihilation of a weak and sick race is far more humanitarian as compared to their protection. Additionally, Hitler observed that the destruction of "the weak and sick race" would provide more space for "the strong." Backed by Hitler's illusions, the Nazis formed two main concepts: Greater Lebensraum (living space), which called for territorial expansion, and the German ethnic power.

Mein Kampf

The *Mein Kampf* was the book that changed the Nazis' view about Jews, and propelled Hitler's rise to power.

In the early days leading to the growth of Hitler, he maintained a strong dislike for the Jews, blaming them for most of the problems that Germany faced. In his time as an inmate, Hitler came up with the idea of putting his thoughts, ideas, and vision for the new Germany in paper. Thus, he started writing a memoir.

Many would argue that Hitler wrote the book *My Struggle* (translated). However, the truth is that he did not. Instead, Hitler dictated his thoughts to Rudolf Hess in his prison cell, and, later, at Berchtesgaden.

Reading the *Mein Kamp* brings an illusion of Hitler talking about his life and his plans for the "new Germany." At first, Hitler chose "Four and a Half Years of Struggle against Lies, Stupidity, and Cowardice" as the title of the book. However, his publisher shortened the title to *Mein Kampf*, which translates to *My Struggle* or *My Battle*.

In the book, Hitler portrays his inhumane character by categorizing people based on their race and other physical aspects. The book established classes, with Aryans deemed the most superior and of pure quality. Hitler describes the Aryan as the most complete and supreme of all human races. Following Hitler's thinking of Aryan superiority, he argues that there exists an inferior race. At the bottom of the chain lies the Jews, Roma, and other non-Aryans. From the book excerpt, Hitler says;

"...it [Nazi philosophy] by no means believes in an equality of races, but along with their difference, it recognizes their higher or lesser value and feels itself obligated to promote the victory of the better and stronger, and demand the subordination of the inferior and weaker in accordance with the eternal will that dominates this universe."

He continues in other chapters to talk of the Aryan superiority as compared to other races:

"All the human culture, all the results of art, science, and technology that we see before us today, are almost exclusively the creative product of the Aryan... Hence, it is no accident that the first cultures arose in places where the Aryan, in his encounters with lower peoples, subjugated them and bent them to his will. They then became the first technical instrument in the service of a developing culture."

Hitler continues to support his doctrine by stating that the dominated people reap the benefits of being subjugated by being near their masters (the Aryans). The proximity offers the "weak" people an opportunity to learn firsthand from the superior race (Aryan). Hitler attempts to contain the "pollution" of the Aryan race by issuing warnings. Hitler indicates that the Aryans will remain excellent. However, he urges them to avoid interacting freely and intermarrying with the "weaker" ethnic group. Only then will they preserve their "master" status.

The book clearly shows Hitler's resentment toward the Jewish community. Hitler contends that the Jews are conspiring to prevent the Aryans from assuming its rightful position as rulers of the world, by contaminating its racial and cultural purity. The Jews, he says, create structures of governments that require the Aryans to believe in equality and fail to become aware of their racial dominance.

"The mightiest counterpart to the Aryan is represented by the Jew."

The book further portrays Hitler's thoughts about the struggle to dominate the world as a continuing racial, cultural, and political encounter, pitting the Aryans against the Jews. The ideologies of Hitler are detailed in the book. He condemns the Jews for a global conspiracy to take control of the finances of the world. Hitler adds that the Jews have plans to control the media. He also accuses the Jews of creating copious democracy, e.g., communalism.

According to Hitler, the Jews are responsible for encouraging prostitution and other vices. The book further states that the Jews intend to take advantage of the ethos to spread conflict.

Hitler uses the book to spread hatred for the Jews by referring to them as: Vermin, fibbers, murky, cunning, nifty, devious, and shrewd, without any authentic culture, a parasite, a broker, a young insect, eternal bloodsuckers, nauseating, dishonest, brutes, alien, threat, cruel, greedy, the destructive force to Aryan humanity, and the earthly foe of Aryan humanity, etc.

"...for the higher he climbs, the more alluring the old goal that was once promised him rises from the veil of the past, and with feverish avidity, his keenest minds see the dream of world domination tangibly approaching."

In the end, the Nazis would adopt Hitler's conspiracy theory and the concept of "competition" for the domination of the world between Jews and Aryans, using it as a just cause to exterminate the Jews. Together with Hitler's ethnic assertiveness toward the Jews, the ideology would spread all over Germany and beyond to other German-occupied territories. The doctrine shared would drive their ambitions to exterminate the Jews as active members of the Nazi party.

Apart from the call for the extermination of the Jews, *Mein Kampf* offers explanations for the military assaults that Hitler and the larger Germany would later launch. Hitler holds the view that the master race is entitled to vast land and "living space," acquired by force or naturally given. The idea would drive his ambition to consolidate more Lebensraum (living space) through armed assaults on Poland, Belgium, the Soviet Union, and the Netherlands.

To achieve this status, Hitler states, "Germany must first overthrow its old foe, France." This plan is seen as a revenge mission for the First World War, in which Hitler felt that the Germans were humiliated. Hitler desperately makes an account of the events in which he supposes Germany was being denied victory by the in-house forces.

In the second volume of the *Mein Kampf*, Hitler puts the blame entirely on the Jews, warning the "pure" Germans of the Jewish treachery.

When the book was first published, it had a low score in terms of sales. The text failed to fulfill the anticipation of the people who expected the tales from Hitler's failed coup attempt. Additionally, the language mastery was poor, depicting a half-educated man. However, when Hitler was made the chancellor of Germany in 1933, the books sold millions of copies. The Nazis considered it an integral part of their life, and the war against their enemies. *Mein Kampf* was availed in schools, and was thought of as a deserving gift to the people of Germany who shared a common philosophy. Bearing in mind the degree of disclosure the book had, Hitler later showed regret producing it. The revelations reflected the character of Hitler and his master plans for the "new Germany" community, plans he'd, instead, keep secret.

Hitler's War Against the Jews

The Nazi leader, Adolf Hitler, had vile detestation for the Jews, terming them as impurities to the German superiority, and cancer on the German community. The views are, however, dubbed by the Holocaust survivor, Saul Friedlander, as "redemptive anti-Semitism." He further states that Hitler aimed at restoring Germany from societal ills and plagues that infested its social and political sphere. Nonetheless, Hitler opposed the Jewish values that threatened the superiority of the Germans. The Jews supported the notions of societal impartiality and sympathetic support of the helpless. The two proved a threat to Hitler's ideology of restoring the natural order, which is the extermination of the weak (dependent) species. In Hitler's world, the dominant race exercised uninhibited power over the "inferior" race. He developed the idea that, when such forces are restrained, the mighty are destabilized, infested, and become impure.

What is termed as a "war against the Jews" started with Hitler's need to expand the territories of Germany to secure food and other resources, which were very limited in Europe. In the aftermath of the First World War, the Allied forces had denied Germany colonial territories in Africa. Hitler's first resolution when he rose to power in 1933 was to abolish governmental disapproval and to consolidate power. Restructuring Germany began with a war against the Jewish community. The Nazis imposed an embargo on Jewish business in April 1933. Days later, the Jewish population in the civil service experienced a reduction, and by the start of May 1933, German schools became a restricted zone from Jewish participation. The events that followed saw Nazi students storming public libraries and bookstores to remove books that were contrasting the Nazi philosophy, and those whose authors were not Aryans. To symbolically cleanse the German culture, the students, together with their lecturers, burned the books in the open fire.

"Where one burns books, one will, in the end, burn people," said Heinrich Heine.

As foreshadowed by a German-Jew poet, it took the Nazis approximately eight years, since the burning of the books, to start burning the Jews.

Extermination of the Jews

The destruction of Jews started with the requirement of German Law to distinguish the Aryans from the Jews. The provision sought to safeguard the blood, honor, and regulations of the Reich Citizens. The Law became a pillar of discernment against the Jews. The Law prohibited intermarriages between German of Jewish origin and

"Pure-blooded" Germans. The regulation also gave Germans civil and political rights at the expense of the Jews.

Phase 1: Categorization

The classification of Germans and Jews can be said to be the first phase that ushered the destruction of the Jews. The Nurnberg Law officially categorized German and Jews. Though the Law never gave a clear definition of German or Jew, it built a wall between the two races. The Law did not consider Jews as a religious group, but a weak race that did not deserve similar treatment to other Germans. In November 1933, the Law created two basic categories of Jews: The first category consisted of the Jews with not less than three grandparents, and the Jew population with two or fewer grandparents (also referred to as "mongrels"). The description gave a controversial definition of a "Jew", rooted not on the identity or religion, but the bloodline.

Phase 2: The Resistance

In response to the rise of Hitler, the Jews saw it necessary to protect their dignity as Germans. Jew journalist, Robert Weltsch, urged his fellow Jews to "wear their identity with pride." As part of the German troops that fought in the First World War, the Jews found it devastating to be considered lesser Germans. The reactions intensified by the end of 1933, seeing a rise of Zionist activism. Other formidable personalities expressed their displeasure, leading their folks to resist the Nazis' oppression of the Jews. Martin Buber, a devout Jewish thinker, called for the Jewish adult education in what he termed as "preparations for the long journey ahead." Another Jew leader, Rabbi Leo Baeck, spread prayer for the day of the atonement, which had a message of resistance. Leo Baeck stated, "We bow down before G-d; we stand erect before man." As much as few Jews foresaw the outcome of the resistance, none would imagine how dangerous it would be. The Jews failed to appeal for help.

By the end of 1939, many Jews were at the end of their rope to find states of asylum. A few were lucky to get visas to emigrate to the

United States of America and Palestine, which opened doors for Jew refugees. Other countries, however, were not willing to let in a large number of refugees, which proved a challenge. In response to the plea of Jewish refugees, the United States of America and other European nations met in France to solve the problem. Then U.S. president, Franklin D. Roosevelt (did not attend), invited other heads of states to welcome the resettlement program. He noted that the rules would not have to amend their laws or devote government resources toward the plan, but only use charitable funds for the resettlement program. In the end, the states made less effort in resettling the Jews.

With the failed plan to seek refuge in other countries, the Jews were left at the mercy of the Nazi extremists. In 1938, the Nazis coordinated an anti-Jewish attack throughout the Reich (including Austria). In less than two days, the Nazis had set ablaze, looted, or damaged synagogues and ruined Jewish businesses. More than 25,000 Jewish men were arrested and confined in concentration camps. The discernment of the Jews was evident among other members of the society as the police watched the riots without offering assistance and firefighters managing the raging fire to prevent spread to adjacent Aryan businesses. In the end, the Jews accepted their fate: They did not have a future in Germany.

Phase 3: Oppressive Laws and Restrictions

In a more contradictory sense, the Jewish population was made to pay a fine of one billion Reichsmarks for the damage caused to the German economy. Furthermore, the Jews were forced to clean up the cost of the riot. Other restraining laws were labeled on the Jewish community. The law prohibited the collection of insurance money by the German Jews. A restraining order was put in place, barring the Jew population from famous social grounds. They were made to shun German schools and travel in isolated cubicles in trains. The severe restrictions were coupled with the earlier bans that closed the door for Jews to earn university degrees, own a business, or practice law and medicine to serve the non-Jew population. In a program dubbed the "Aryanization," the Nazis continued to seize the properties of the Jews. The atrocities faced by the Jews can be summed up by the Goring phrase:

"I would not like to be a Jew in Germany!"

Victims of the Nazis' Brutality

As much as the Jews were at the center of the Nazis' extermination agenda, other people also faced the atrocities. The target group stretched far beyond the Jews. Some people were persecuted for going against the central ideologies of the Nazis, while others were killed for refusing to take part in the Nazi programs. Social egalitarians, political rebels, and trade unionists were the first group of people to be arrested and confined in the concentration camps.

The Nazis also imprisoned more than twenty thousand Jehovah's Witness members for failing to swear allegiance to the state and Hitler. The detainees were, however, given the option of renouncing their faith in exchange for their freedom. Few opted for apostasy, while the majority chose martyrdom.

The Nazis also targeted Germans of African descent (mostly called the "Rhineland bastards"). These were the offspring of German mothers and French African troops who occupied the Rhineland after the First World War. The persecutions were less methodical. However, the Nazis forcefully sterilized them. The Nazis held the view that the German of African origin would multiply and "pollute" the population, thus diminishing the "pure" German race. The Roma and Sinti (Gypsies) were also singled out. The two groups were also gassed in concentration camps. Roma and Sinti were also termed "racial polluters." Their delineation as being asocial was the justification for their maltreatment and massacre.

The Euthanasia Program

After the beginning of the Second World War, the Germans instigated the T4 Program, also known as the "Euthanasia program". The plan was aimed at "wiping out" all people living with disabilities in Germany. This lot disturbed Hitler's ideology of Aryan supremacy. These Germans were termed as "useless eaters" and "unworthy of life." The Nazis cited financial rationalization as the reason for their persecution. The use of gas chambers and crematoria were conventional methods of oppression in the T4 Program.

The German mass protested the killings. Many religious leaders, such as Clemens August (Roman Catholic bishop), detested the program, forcing it to stop. However, the Nazis continued to secretly persecute people with disabilities.

The policy of German on occupation targeted the Jews and non-Jewish Poles, following the invasion of Poland. Hitler's pursuit of "village space" sought to put an end to the Polish community and nationhood. The Nazis exterminated Polish religious leaders and legislators. They demolished the Polish governance and abducted the children of selected Polish. The children were brought up as "voluntary Aryans" by their new German "parents." Many Poles were also forced into hard and compulsory labor on survival diets. Some were dispossessed of their properties and evacuated, and were incarcerated in concentration camps.

The Expansion of German and Formation of Ghettoes

In contradiction to the German policy of exterminating Jews and getting rid of the Jewish community in Germany, the territorial expansion brought more Jews under the control of Germany. The annexation of Austria and Sudetenland (currently in the Czech Republic) brought more Jews under the supervision of Germany. The invasion led to more assaults. The "Jewish question" became an urgent matter, following the invasion of Poland. More than two million Jews came under the control of Germany after the division of Poland between Germany and the Soviet Union. As the need to get rid of the Jews intensified, the Nazis thought of deporting the Jewish population to the island of Madagascar. However, due to the scarcity of resources required for the deportation, the Nazis abandoned the idea as unrealistic. Additionally, the war on the sea poised a threat to Germany, which had not triumphed in the Battle of Britain. Entering the waters would mean going to a war they had already lost.

The growing Jewish population saw the creation of the Jewish council by Reinhardt Heydrich in 1939. The council comprised of 24 rabbis and Jewish leaders. The council was made answerable to the German leadership and to carry out German orders. With the establishment of the Warsaw Ghetto (the largest ghetto in Poland), the Jewish population was confined to less than three percent of the city area, despite being the most extensive section of the Warsaw population. The outbreak of disease, hunger, and malnutrition took their toll on the community, even before the first Germany bullet had been fired.

The establishment of ghettoes was viewed as a temporary measure by the German leadership. The ghettoes were meant to confine the Jews until a lasting solution to their population was found. On the other hand, the Jews thought that they would be enclosed in the ghettoes until the end of the Second World War. The Jews thought of making ghetto life endurable even under the most demanding conditions. The Jews found alternatives for the prohibited privileges. They resorted to underground schools when the Nazis barred them from schools. They secretly continued their religious life. They mostly used songs and humor for defiance. Later on, when the atrocities continued, the Jews resorted to armed revolts.

Mass Killings

There existed a specific date for the commencement of the systematic extermination of the Jews. The "final solution to the Jewish question" remains a strategy that no one knows how and when it started (whether it was a unilateral decision or a sequence of deliberated decisions). Nonetheless, the Nazis began the mass extermination of the Jewish population in June 1941 with the attack on the Soviet Union—a former ally of Germany.

Germany deployed a mobile killing unit in the territories of the Soviet Union. The troops were ordered to kill Jews, Soviet commissars, and Roma in the conquered regions. The soldiers were, at times, helped by the local police, native anti-Semitic communities, and associated Axis troops in cornering the victims and dragging them out of town to be shot. The Einsatzgruppe, the killing troop, killed more than thirty-three thousand Jews in Kyiv and the Babi Yar. More Jews (approximately twenty-eight thousand) were murdered in Rumbula Forest, outside the town of Riga, Latvia. Seventy thousand more Jews were killed in Vilna (currently Vilnius). At the Ninth Fort, the troops executed nine thousand Jews, including children. The waves of attack on the Jews continued until the Soviet Union struck a retaliation plan. In the end, the killing units returned to dig up the bodies of the Jews and burn them to destroy evidence of the massacre. The wave of attack was said to have claimed the lives of approximately one and a half million people—mainly Jews. However, the locals also turned on their Jewish neighbors, letting the German troops take the blame for the killings. The presence of German soldiers would, at the time, spur chaos and massacre. In the Baltics, the nationalist bands turned on the Jews, too, killing them in numbers.

Jewish Resistance

Additionally, allies were ready to strike at the slightest provocation and were enthusiastically resolute to see the "final solution" come to fruition. Besides, the Nazis went to greater lengths to conceal their actions to avoid international attention. The German policy of mutual retaliation also made it hard for the Jews in the ghettoes to resist.

However, the situation changed when Germany finally ordered the closure of the ghettoes, making the Jew community aware of the imminent death that awaited them. The Jew community decided to stage a series of resistance in the forests, ghettoes, and the concentration camps. The Jews fought alone, and sometimes, alongside the other resistance groups in Russia, France, and

Yugoslavia. The Jews staged a one-to-one rebellion when they realized their imminent death.

In April 1943, a young Jew, Mordecai Anielewicz, led the Warsaw ghetto uprising, following mass deportation of the Jews to the concentration camp in Treblinka. Elsewhere in Vilna, realizing the intentions of the German policies toward the Jew, Abba Kovner mounted armed resistance from December 1941. Kovner led the revolt in fighting the Germans throughout September 1943. In March 1943, the gay community, sympathizers, and activists led by Willem Arondeus bombed the registry in Amsterdam to destroy lists of Jews and other people hunted by the Nazis. Similar to the Warsaw ghetto uprising, Treblinka and Sobibor also staged uprisings in fear of their lives in the extermination camps. Just as the killing was coming to an end in 1944, the "special commando" unit in Auschwitz demolished a crematorium.

With the advancing of the allied forces in 1944, the Nazis, mostly the security services officials in the death camps, desperately tried to evacuate the camps and conceal their actions. Desperate to avoid leaving evidence behind, the security services moved the inmates westward, forcing them to march to the core of the German territory. There were more than fifty "death marches" from the extermination camps as the Nazi domination slowly came to an end. The inmates were offered meager or no food and water and were not allowed to rest along the way. The ones who fell behind or could not continue with the march were shot instantly.

Days before the arrival of the red army in Auschwitz, the Nazis marched more than sixty thousand people to Wodzisław, and put them on cargo trains (mostly in open cars) to the Holocaust death camps at Gross-Rosen, Dachau, Mauthausen, and Buchenwald. Statistics show that one in four succumbed on the way. In April and May of 1945, American and British forces, on their way to soldierly objectives, entered the death camps in the west and witnessed what had transpired. Although tens of thousands of inmates had perished, the camps were far from the utmost lethal. Still, even for the battle-weary militaries who supposed they had, at present, comprehended the vilest, the sights and whiffs and the wasted survivors they came upon left an ineffaceable memory.

The conditions of the prisoners were so vile that some died after being freed. At Dachau, the soldiers came across railway cars fit to burst with dead bodies. In some camps, the soldiers had set them ablaze to control the spread of typhus. For the survivors, their freedom never seemed like moments of triumph. Viktor Frankl, a survivor of Auschwitz, recalls:

"Everything was unreal. Unlikely as in a dream. Only later—and for some, it was very much later or never—was liberation liberating."

The allied governments who had received prior information about the carnage made no military attempt to rescue the Jews. The allied forces did not bomb the railway tracks leading to the concentration camps. For the allies, the war at hand was very crucial, and only after victory could they get involved in rescuing the Jews. No noticeable action was embarked on explicitly to end the extermination. And then an internal memo from a U.S. general counsel to the U.S. Secretary of the Treasury, Henry Morgenthau, branded the policy of the U.S. state department an "acquiescence to the murder of the European Jews." Following the condemnation, criticism, and the memo, Morgenthau facilitated the establishment of the War Refugee Board, making a late and inadequate attempt to liberate dying out Jews, primarily through international relations and stratagem.

Chapter 3: Events Leading to the Attack

Historical Anti-Semitism and the Rise of Adolf Hitler

Long before the Holocaust, there existed evidence of hostility toward the Jews. A good example is the destruction of Jewish synagogues and forceful eviction out of Palestine by the Romans. However, at the time, while there existed massive support for the Jewish population, the educated elite advocated for religious tolerance.

Additionally, the reign of Napoleon saw a change in legislation that put an end to Jewish restrictions. Other European leaders also followed suit in the 17th and 18th centuries. Despite all these efforts, anti-Semitic ideologies continued to spread across Europe. The discernment followed the racial path rather than the religious path. The cases are evidence that the hatred toward the Jew community did not start with the reign of Hitler. However, Hitler remains a compelling character in the spread of the ideology.

Literature and history do not provide the origin of the predominantly vile type of anti-Semitism adopted by Hitler and the Nazis. However, a shallow understanding has, in the past, been drawn from Hitler's time as a prisoner. Hitler was born in Austria in the year 1889, and served as a member of the German troop that was involved in the First World War. Hitler, like most Germans, blamed the Jewish population for the defeat of Germany in the war. At the end of the First World War, Hitler joined the German Workers' Party and later renamed it to the currently-known Nazis. His involvement in the Beer Hall Putsch in 1923 landed him in prison for treason charges. While in prison, he wrote a memoir, *Mein Kampf*. In his book, Hitler forecasted the annihilation of the Jewish race in Germany.

Hitler's aggression toward the Jews was based on his obsession with the idea of "pure German superiority" and the need to create enough space for the Nazis. A decade after his release, Hitler banked on the weaknesses of his rivals to strengthen the status of the Nazis and ultimately rise to power. Hitler was named the chancellor of Germany in January 1933, and further anointed himself as the supreme ruler of Germany, following the death of President Paul Von Hindenburg in 1934.

The Nazi Revolution

At the center of Hitler's regime were the ideas of German racial purity and the expansion strategy. The designs were incorporated in the year 1933, when he rose to power, intending to implement foreign and domestic policies. In his first days, the Nazi supremacist only served harsh prosecutions to the opposition leaders and the communists. The call to wipe out opposition in German saw the construction of the first concentration camp in Dachau in March 1933. The camp served as a prison for communists and other opposition generals.

Dachau became a killing ground under the guard of Heinrich Himmler. By July of that year, other concentration camps had already been constructed to house communists, rebels, and foreigners. Later on, the Nazis came up with the "Aryanization" strategy, aimed at removing foreigners, mostly Jews from the civil service, clearing up Jewish businesses, and robbing Jewish lawyers and doctors of their clients. The Nuremberg Law was established to categorize Jews and half-breeds.

The Law became a weapon of Jew stigmatization, cruelty, and maltreatment. The bad blood culminated on the "night of broken glass", where Jewish businesses were burned, windows broken, and synagogues destroyed. On that day, hundreds of Jews were killed, and thousands were arrested.

The Beginning of the War

The beginning of the war was marked by the German invasion of Poland in 1939. In the yeas to follow, German troops forced thousands of Polish Jews from their homes and confined them in ghettos. The seized possessions of the Jews were given to other Germans (those who lived outside Germany) and polish gentiles. High walls surrounded the confinement ghettos and were used as incarceration of city-states. The Jewish Councils governed the ghettos. Due to congestion and inadequate sanitation facilities, the ghettos soon become breeding grounds for diseases, e.g., typhus.

In the late 1930s, the Nazis officially set up the 'Euthanasia' program, which saw the gassing to death of more than seventy thousand Germans diagnosed with cerebral disorders. Hitler was forced to shut the program in 1941 by protests of German religious leaders. However, his troops continued to massacre people with disabilities behind closed doors. The death toll hit an approximate two hundred and seventy-five thousand by 1945. The perception after the fact is that the Euthanasia program championed the beginning of the Holocaust.

The Beginning of the "Final Solution"

The German troops led successful expansion missions across Europe throughout the year 1940, under the leadership of Hitler. They conquered Denmark, Norway, Netherlands, Belgium, France, and Luxembourg. With the expeditions underway, Jews from all over Europe, and other European Gypsies were transported and confined in Polish ghettoes. The beginning of the final solution was experienced in June 1941, when Germany invaded the Soviet Union, killing more than half a million people in the process. The German troops used mobile units to attack, by shooting, the Soviet Jews.

On July 31, 1941, Hitler's top commander, Hermann Goering, drafted a memorandum to the chief of the security service, outlining the need to have the final solution to "the Jewish question." What followed was the tagging of all Jews with a yellow star, exposing them to the waiting danger. The vents culminated in the deportation of the Jews to Polish ghettoes and other cities occupied by German in the USSR.

The beginning of June 1941 saw experimental killings in the concentration camps—mainly the Auschwitz. German doctors experimented with the effectiveness of specific therapeutic methods, using the Jews as guinea pigs. In August, German officials used a pesticide, Zyklon-B, to gas more than five hundred Soviet Jews to death. The security service at that time ordered the pesticide in bulk—a threatening pointer of the Holocaust to come.

Holocaust Death Camps

The beginning of the Holocaust death camps was marked by the transportation of the Jews from the ghettoes to special concentration camps. The deportation from the ghettoes was carried out in an organized manner. The troops identified the mostly perceived as weak, sick, and young for the first lot of transportation. In 1942-1945, the Jewish community faced deportation in massive numbers to the concentration camps from all over the continent, including all the states allied to Germany. The deportation program led to the emergence of the Warsaw Ghetto Uprising in 1943. Warsaw Ghetto inhabitants rose to arms in revolt against the system, which brought diseases and hunger to the people. The rebellion ended in the death of more than seven thousand Jews. More than fifty thousand Jews who survived the aftermath of the revolt were sent to concentration camps. The Warsaw Ghetto revolt inspired mass revolts in many camps and ghettos across Germany and the entire continent.

At first, the Nazis maintained the mass killings a secret. However, the massive number of victims made it impossible to conceal for a long time. The survivors and eyewitnesses who successfully escaped the camps took the news of the killings across Europe, getting the attention of the Allied Forces. The Allied Governments would later face massive criticism for their failure to respond or make the news of the mass killings in the concentration camps public. The Allied forces were, at the time, so much focused on winning the war. However, the governments have since given their reasons for failing to act. The Allied Governments cited widespread skepticism of the Holocaust news, coupled with the repudiation and uncertainty that such carnages could occur, and in such a large number.

The most notorious and the largest extermination camp, Auschwitz, was built in a three-structure design. The prison camp (Auschwitz I), an extermination camp (Auschwitz II–Birkenau), and a slave labor camp (Auschwitz III–Buna-Monowitz). On arrival to Auschwitz, the Jews went through a selection process. A German doctor headed the selection process. The process was meant to separate children, pregnant women, the sick, the elderly, and the well-built, healthy Jews. The healthy Jews were taken into forced labor, while the rest faced immediate extermination.

The factories adjacent to the Auschwitz, such as IG Farben, enjoyed the vast availability of workforce and invested intensively in the process. The corporation assumed that forced labor would be a lasting section of the economy. The Jewish were worked to death, with no food, shelter, clothing, or medical attention. On occasions, the Germans would perform another selection exercise, and transfer the slaves who could work to the gas chambers of Birkenau. Unlike the camps of Auschwitz and Majdanek, which used prisoners to offer support to the Germany involvement in the war, the campsites at Belzec, Treblinka, and Sobibor were solely killing zones.

The most astonishing camp massacre occurred in Auschwitz. Approximately 2 million individuals lost their lives in Auschwitz alone in a method reminiscent of an extensive industrialized process. The Auschwitz housed both Jews and non-Jew prisoners. However, only the Jew population was gassed in the process. A large number also succumbed to diseases and hunger. In the year 1943, eugenicist Josef Mengele visited the Auschwitz to carry out several medical experiments. The physician, also named the "Angel of Death", experimented on Jewish inmates, mostly twins, through injections.

The events leading to the Holocaust in dates:

- January 30, 1933: Hitler's appointment as the chancellor of Germany

On this date, President Hindenburg invited Hitler to resume the office of the Chancellor of Germany, following provisional voting.

- February 27, 1933: The Reichstag fire

  The parliament in berlin is set ablaze. The Nazi government declares a state of emergency following the fire incident, and arrests and executes a Dutch radical, Marinus van der Lubbe.

- March 5, 1933: The Reichstag Elections

  Following the burning of the parliament, a parliamentary election was conducted in March 1933. The Nazis gained 44% votes. The exercise was undemocratic, since many opposition leaders had already been exiled.

- March 22, 1933: The establishment of Dachau

  A concertation camp is established in Dachau near Munich to house political prisoners, mostly communists. The following day, the Enabling Act is passed, to grant the government dictatorial powers for four years.

- April 1, 1933: The Boycott

  On this day, the Nazi government declares a nationwide boycott of all Jewish-owned businesses. The boycott marks the first mass action against the Jews.

- April 7, 1933: The reforms in the civil service

  The Nazi regime passes a law to reform the public service. Jews are barred from the civil service. President Hindenburg excuses the Jew front-line soldiers of the First World War from the ban.

- May 10, 1933: Burning of books

Nazi students and their professors storm into libraries and bookstores. They remove all the books written by Jews and other non-Aryans, and publicly set them ablaze.

- July 11, 1933: Sterilization Law

  The Nazi government passes a law to prevent people with disabilities and other hereditary diseases to multiply. The ruling came into effect in 1934, seeing more than four hundred thousand people sterilized.

- September 22: The law on the Reich Chamber of Culture

  A bill is passed, banning Jews and other non-Aryans from participating in German cultures. The law prohibits Jews from theatres and other public events.

- August 2, 1934: The death of Hindenburg

  German President Paul von Hindenburg dies. Following the death, Hitler anoints himself as the Reichsfuehrer—the supreme ruler of Germany.

- September 15, 1935: Anti-Semitic Law

  Hitler declares the anti-Semitic Nuremberg Laws at a Nazi rally. The Nuremberg Laws are made up of two separate regulations, namely the Law for the 'Protection of German Blood and German Honor' and the 'Reich Citizenship' Law.

- July 12, 1936: Another concentration camp

  The second concentration camp is established in Oranienburg, near Berlin, acting as an incarceration center. A third camp would later be installed on July 15, 1937, at Buchenwald.

- March 12, 1938:The annexation of Austria

On this date, German troops invade and annex Austria. More than two hundred thousand Jews in Austria are subjected to the same anti-Semitic laws as German Jews.

- June 14, 1938: Compulsory registration of Jewish businesses

  The Nazi government declares that all businesses owned by the Jews must be registered and marked as 'Jewish'. The day that follows sees the arrest of "asocial" Jews. Any Jew who had a previous arrest record is arrested and transported to the death camps at Buchenwald, Dachau, and Sachsenhausen.

- November 9, 1938: The pogrom

  On the nights of 9th and 10th November, the Nazis invade Jewish businesses, breaking the windows and looting. Synagogues are sullied and demolished. Many Jews are killed, and others arrested and confined in concentration camps. Five days later, all Jewish children are expelled from German schools.

- September 1, 1938: Operation T4

  On this date, Hitler authorizes operation 'Euthanasia'. People with disabilities are captured and killed, including children. The program is halted, but secretly continues until 1945, when the war ends.

- November 23, 1939: All Jews in Poland are forced to wear an armband, showing a yellow Star of David in public.
- October 16, 1940: The establishment of the Warsaw Ghetto

  The Warsaw Ghetto, the largest of the Jewish ghettoes, was established in 1940. The ghetto was later sealed on November 15, 1940.

- March 1, 1941: Construction of Auschwitz-Birkenau

  The structure of the second part of the Auschwitz (Birkenau) begun on March 1, 1941. This section ended up becoming the most crowded and brutal part of the camp. Most of the gassing and burning of the Jews took place in this wing of the Auschwitz. On September 22, 1941, the first gassing experiment took place in Auschwitz. The concentration camp of Belzec would later be established on November 1 of the same year.

- July 15 to October 28: Deportations

  In between the dates, Jews were deported from Amsterdam, the Warsaw ghetto, and Theresienstadt, to the several extermination camps—mainly the Auschwitz and the Treblinka.

- April 19, 1943: The Warsaw Ghetto uprising

  Following mass deportation to the extermination camps, and the final phases of liquidating the Warsaw ghetto, the Jews staged an armed revolt in the streets. The Germans, however, began burning the ghetto the day that followed, shooting any Jew that attempted to run away from the burning houses. The Warsaw resistance would later inspire similar uprising at Treblinka on August 2, 1943.

- On January 17, 1945, the Soviet Union army would come to the rescue, liberating the remaining seven thousand five hundred inmates from Auschwitz.

Part II: Living to Tell the Story—Survivor Stories

After getting an idea of what the Holocaust was all about, let's now delve into the personal experiences of some survivors. Perhaps this can provide us with some deeper insights regarding the atrocities committed against them while in detention at the Auschwitz concentration camp. Shall we? You can read that in the following chapters.

Chapter 4: The Story of Irene Fogel Weiss

Irene Fogel Weiss was born on November 21, 1930, in Bótrágy, Czechoslovakia, currently known as Batrad, Ukraine. Her parents were Leah Fogel and Meyer. During her younger days, her mother was a housewife, while her father, Meyer, ran a family lumber yard. Money from sales enabled her parents to raise them. She had five siblings, namely: Reuven, Moshe, Serena, Edit, and Gershon.

Bótrágy was a tiny township located in Czechoslavakia, with an approximated population of one thousand individuals that included about ten Jewish families. Her childhood was defined by poverty, just like her surroundings. Most of her neighbors practiced farming as their only source of livelihood. Other than that, small-time income-generating activities like vegetable selling, tailoring, and shoemaking dominated the township. Due to their close proximity and familiarity, people in that township related well.

After the Holocaust, she migrated to New York in 1947, and got married to Martin Weiss in 1949. And, by 1953, they had relocated to Northern Virginia. She thereafter enrolled for a Bachelor of Arts degree in Education at an American University, which enabled her to teach at the Fairfax public school, Virginia, for thirteen years. Currently, she and her husband Martin have three children and four grandchildren, and she is also a volunteer at the U.S. Holocaust Memorial Museum. On the other hand, her elder sister currently resides in New Jersey.

Her Ordeal

Trouble started at her home tuft (Bótrágy) approximately in 1938. She was eight years old by then. Her township had been annexed by Hungary after her country had been torn apart. Hungary, being a German-affiliate nation, perpetrated anti-Semitic ideologies toward the Jew population that existed in their newfound land. Consequently, all the Jews, including her family, were subjected to ridicule and mistreatment from the marauding Nazis. There was no existent law to protect them and their property. As a result, most of it was looted and given to the non-Jews. For instance, her father's lumber business was taken from him and given to a non-Jew.

Furthermore, they were discriminated in most places, and were unable to use public amenities, such as schools, trains, and public grounds, due to the violence and hatred directed toward them. As a result, they cowered before other races, so as not to bring attention to themselves. Donning a yellow star was a requirement for them so that they could be easily identified, which made them prone to frequent beatings from the other races.

Also, many men of Jewish origin numbering in thousands were forcefully recruited to labor groups, which worked under the supervision of the army in 1942. Irene's father was amongst them, and after a period of six months, he came back home to find the Jew population being subjected to much harsher living conditions.

By 1944, the Hungarian government had not yet handed over its Jewish population to the Auschwitz concentration camp. As such, the Nazis were forced to invade Hungary and bark out orders for them to round up all the Jew population and deport them to the camp. And these sealed the fate of the Jewish population residing in Hungary, which included Irene's family. Therefore, in April 1944,

45

they were herded up like animals and taken to Munkács ghetto, which was a transit point aboard cattle vehicles.

However, this place wasn't designed to hold people; it was a brick manufacturing plant. Thus, thousands of people were subjected to squalid living conditions. They were overcrowded, and the only restroom they had was a trench dug outside the factory. Upon arrival, girls who were less than sixteen years of age were immediately shaved; Irene was one of them. However, her mother gave her a headscarf to cover her bald head, which would later save her life during the selection phase at the Auschwitz concentration camp. It would make her look older than her age.

From Munkács ghetto, they were transported to Auschwitz using similar carts they had come with. Within a period of two months, at least four hundred and twenty-five thousand Jews had been deported from Hungary to Auschwitz.

What hurt her most was how inhuman and sudden the deportation was. People who had existed together and known each other for decades were rudely and abruptly separated without sufficient notice. Furthermore, they were only allowed to leave with a single suitcase that was meant to carry all their earthly belongings; it was devastating. She vividly remembered the night her mother struggled to park their belongings inside a bag. They were too many to the extent that made her pack and unpack several times. In frustration, she left all the other things and only packed beddings, prepared food, and warm cloth. Then it was full. As a measure, she took the wedding ring, a watch, and several earrings that they would use to trade for food if the opportunity arose. The following day, they were herded to the town hall where her father was told to surrender all his cash to a group comprising of the school principal and mayor.

Auschwitz was beyond her imagination for the few years she had lived on Earth, and was a complete opposite of what she had been accustomed to. Due to her young age, she was completely devastated and scared with what she saw, and wondered why they were being taken there, or what mistakes they had done to warrant such treatment. At first, her father thought that it was a work camp, due to the uniforms, barracks, and prisoners he could see, and was a bit encouraged, since he heard stories of the Jews being shot in Poland. Therefore, working as a prisoner was at least a welcoming option.

At first, they thought to themselves that it was a form of discrimination. These people did not know how they would be affected. The Germans had hatched a meticulous genocide plan that they were unaware of. As such, they didn't anticipate the murder of Jewish children to terminate the growth of its population.

With no other options left on their hands at that moment, the majority of them resigned to fate; however, they had the hopes of seeing each other around. Sadly, that was not going to be the case. On their part, the Germans skillfully employed deceptive tactics to lure their targets. For instance, they made the Jewish think that they were being recruited for labor work, but in reality, it's extermination through work, and going for a shower, but in reality, it's going into a slaughterhouse, among other things.

On their arrival, her family was divided. Her older brother and father were taken to one side, her younger siblings and mother to the other side, and her sister on another side. She couldn't help but hold on to her younger sister, momentarily. Eventually, she was directed to her mother's side, while she headed to the other side where her elder sister was, giving her the first chance of survival.

Unknown to them, they were being photographed, which was an order from above. Photographs of Hungarian Jews arriving at the platform and their moments when receiving prison attires and heading to the bath were taken.

The discovery of such photographs enabled her to identify herself at the arrival platform after she had been separated from her sister. In a different photograph, she can identify her family heading to the gas chamber. Some of the family members in the photo were her mother and her two younger brothers. The picture of her arrival was published some twenty-five years later in a book entitled *The Auschwitz Album* by Yad Vashem, and was brought to her by her daughter. According to her, everything in the picture is a true portrayal of what had transpired during her time at the concentration camp.

Her father was selected to do labor as *sonderkommando*, which entailed the removal of dead bodies from the slaughterhouses (gas chambers) and setting them on fire. It was routine for the SS personnel at the camp to execute the *sonderkommandos* after some period and to replace them with new arrivals. She came to realize later, through her aunt, that her father had been shot dead after refusing to perform his duties as a *sonderkommando*.

Some of the psychological traumas meant to humiliate them during their arrival happened at the processing centers. Here, the women were stripped naked, then shaved of all their hair, including the pubic area, by the Jewish men. In Irene's perspective, the Nazis wanted to humiliate and kill the Jews without involving any morality in the process. After fumbling around, trying to locate her sister, she remembered being taken ahead of the line into the shower room, then told to find her sister among the other shaved faces. Everyone looked the same to her every time a new door was opened.

After meeting, talking, and asking questions about the whereabouts of her brothers, sister, and parents to several people who had arrived before her, they simply showed her the chimneys. At first, she did not take any of their words seriously, but it did not take her long to understand and accept whatever was taking place. Her station near the crematorium gave her a vantage position of witnessing thousands of innocent children, women, and men lining up for the gas chambers without knowing what was going to happen to them. Most of them were killed within less than an hour after their arrival, and their bodies were cremated.

During their time of arrival, the crematorium was operating full time, thus consuming thousands of Hungarian Jews. She was lucky to be enlisted as a slave worker, together with her elder sister, Serena, and they were stationed at the Birkenau section of the concentration camp. They stayed together for most of the period, amid threats to separate them.

Another comforting thing amid all the craziness that was going around is that they were able to meet their younger aunts. They were Piri and Rose, who were barely into their 20s, which made her stop crying within a short period. Meeting their aunts in such a situation motivated and emotionally uplifted them, and provided them with the will to survive.

The four worked in a store known as the "Canada" section, which was a name given to the storage location found next to the crematoria IV. It housed the prisoners' clothes and other belongings. They stayed in this place for the duration of eight months up to January 1985. To get by during that period of eight months, she had to detach herself from the present. All the suffering and horror was too much to hold.

In most cases, she lived as though she was in a dream, and all that was happening wasn't real, and that it would come to an end, and she would survive. She lived in denial. She talks of how they passed the crematorium daily and saw how the *sonderkommandos* pulled gold from the teeth of the dead, and how they were unable to contain the mountain of bodies that were increasing by the day. They also heard the insistent screaming from the gas chambers and the continuous burning of the fire, but chose to remain oblivious and didn't want to believe that anything was happening within their midst. In other instances, she plugged her ears to contain the screaming, and kept telling herself that she would, one day, go home. And what was happening was not in the world that she knew, and it was not her real self that was experiencing whatever was happening.

However, as the Russian troops continued advancing, the Nazis realized that they were at the losing end; therefore, they doubled their killing efforts to wipe out the Jews. At this instance, it became difficult for her not to recognize whatever was happening around them. At that particular time, the crematorium was unable to measure up to the killing speed. These forced the Nazis to burn fresh corpses in the open. Also, the number of items left at the place she was working continued to rise at an alarming speed.

As a result of the Soviet Red Army's advances in January 1945, the SS personnel in charge of the camp initiated a forced match on thousands of prisoners at the camp that led to lots of death. They were being forced to match to Ravensbrück concentration camp that was located inside Germany. What led to most deaths was the fact that the prisoners had no proper clothing for the harsh winter weather that was present at that particular period. Also, most of them were suffering from conditions such as dysentery, typhoid, and starvation. During the march, those lagging due to exhaustion were shot by the SS personnel. Even those stopping to tie their shoelaces or urinate were also shot.

During their transportation later on to Neustadt-Glewe, her aunt, Piri, got sick, which led to her killing. And on another daily morning roll call, her elder sister and a few other slaves were separated from the rest, as they were deemed too thin and weak to engage in any duties. However, Irene told a guard that Serena was her sister, so she needed to join her and was allowed to. The other prisoners who were with them started rumors that they were to be taken back to the main camp to be gassed due to their weak status. Irene and her sister were then contained in a room together with other inmates so that they could wait for transport to the main camp. But, that never materialized.

The advancing Soviet Union forces had caused the SS forces to flee, abandoning the slaves and the camp in their wake. These allowed the prisoners to leave at will. Irene, her aunt Rose, and elder sister took refuge in an empty building in a nearby town. They had to look after themselves, especially after the Russians arrived shortly and left without reason.

The three ladies spent some time trying to reach Prague, where they could find some of their relatives. Here, they found one of their uncles by the name of Joseph Mermelstein. He had left his hometown, gone to Palestine in 1938, and had come back as a soldier. A small number of uncles and aunts had survived the ordeal. However, she and her elder sister, Serena, were the only children who had survived in the whole family.

From Prague, they headed to Teplice-Šanov, Sudetenland. At the start of their stay at the new place, they had no clue what transpired to the other family members, and could not have access to any communication devices, such as a phone. However, the names of the survivors were written on lists, and pinned on most buildings around.

Refugee meetups were characterized with questions regarding where to find relatives and family members. In the process, she ended up finding that out of the one hundred members deported from her town, only ten survived the ordeal. Among the ten were two children.

All the other children and parents were killed at the concentration camp. Upon reaching Sudetenland, her aunt became bedridden due to tuberculosis. Her elder sister got herself a job in a company, while she went to a school in Czech. With financial help from groups, such as the Hebrew Immigrant Aid Society, and support from relatives, she was able to move to New York in the year 1947.

Chapter 5: The Story of David Mermelstein

David Mermelstein, currently eighty-six years old, was born in Kivjazd, Czechoslovakia, in 1928. At the age of fifteen years, he became a Holocaust victim. Like all the other Jews who lived in Hungary after the dismemberment of Czechoslovakia, he was rounded up and deported to Auschwitz-Birkenau. He was among the last half-million individuals to be recruited into the concentration camp. After the ordeal, he was able to make it to America. He was eighteen years of age by then, and went to live in Brooklyn, New York, then proceeded to Rhode Island.

Mermelstein got engaged to his wife in 1948, and eventually got married in 1949. They had their honeymoon at Miami Beach, and it has been a permanent home since then. He has three children, three grandchildren, and a great-grandchild. He is also a member of the Holocaust survivors' foundation, located in the U.S. He strives to ensure that the world never forgets the events that took place during the Holocaust, so that the same can never be repeated in the future.

His Ordeal

David said that he and the rest of the Jews knew nothing about the name "Auschwitz" when they were rounded up. The only idea they had on their minds was that they were being taken to work at a camp. After being taken around through places, such as the Munkács ghetto, they finally arrived at the Auschwitz concentration camp.

On arrival, they were lined in rows of five. Through a wire fence, he could see old women and men with walking sticks, men donning striped pants, playing Jewish songs, and young children playing with balls and dolls, amongst many other activities taking place.

Together with another one hundred prisoners, there was a small wagon belonging to the infamous Dr. Josef Mengele, a man who was known for his cruel experiments on the prisoners at the camp.

He greeted them, then proceeded to conduct the selection process. Donning white gloves on his hands, Dr. Josef Mengele would characteristically look at a prisoner, then motion with a little stick to the left or right, in what was referred to as the selection process. Within seconds, the peoples' fates were determined: Those who are going to be gassed and those who would work to death. And at this time, no prisoner knew what was going to happen to them next. The people who were chosen to die go to the left side; they had to walk a distance of half a mile before reaching the gas chambers and final destination. His younger siblings, parents, and grandparents were sent to the left side, which meant that they were going to die almost immediately upon arriving in the gas chambers.

By stepping on his elder brother's shoes, he was mistaken to be seventeen years old. Thus, he was signaled to move to the right side, in a way saving him from the fate of his other family members. This meant that, together with his brother, he was booked to work at the camp.

Those on the right side, which included him and his brother, were then moved to a room within the barracks, and then instructed to undress. They were provided with new attires to wear, which comprised of a shirt, cap, and pants. They were also advised to retain their shoes only.

On the inquiry of the whereabouts of their family members, a guard directed them to the door and pointed to the chimneys and the smoke emanating from the crematorium and bluntly told them that they no longer had families.

At the camp, attempts by the older arrivals to speak to new arrivals were futile, due to an electric fence that separated them. Anyone attempting to pass a message across was electrocuted. It is at this point that Mermelstein came to understand the meaning of the smoke that continuously emanated from the chimneys.

He also witnessed how a lot of the prisoners electrocuted themselves by holding on to the electric fence. They saw that there was no need for living, so they preferred to die than continue to work until they dropped dead. However, his elder brother living in the same camp discouraged him from doing the same, as it would be assisting the Nazis to accomplish their mission.

As a result, he promised to stay put until the end. His elder brother gave him and his group some survival tactics for their survival. He told them terrible stories of the work camp, where he was placed. For instance, he informed them how they were provided with a single cup of tea in the morning, a piece of potato, and soup for some days during lunch hour. And when they were lucky, they were given a crust of bread for the evening meal. However, the piece was too moldy to be regarded as bread, which made a lot of them sick.

For the remainder of the period at the camp, he struggled to survive by any means, so as not to be sent to the gallows. He did not reveal it when he was sick; he just pretended that nothing was wrong, so as not to be sent to the "hospital" where the prisoners were eventually killed.

In October 1944, according to his estimates, together with other slaves, they were deported to Austria on a forced march that resulted in a massive number of deaths. Upon reaching their destination, he was tasked to work the wagons at a camp known as "Emaze". It was at this place that he discovered that eating coal, which he stole from his workplace, could enable him to reduce hunger pangs.

In his line of duty, a lorry injured his hand and was, therefore, sent to the hospital at the camp. While there, he and the other prisoners came to learn how the outfit operated. Just like the camp where they had come from, those who were sent to the "hospital" never came back. They were only sent there to await their death. Hence, they knew that they had approximately nineteen days remaining for them to be killed and eventually cremated.

Five days to their eventual end, the prisoners at the hospital woke up to a surprise. There were no Germans around the place. An outside check by prisoners who were strong confirmed the absence of the Germans and the free state of the camp. His health had severely deteriorated, and he was on the verge of dying. He could not lift his feet nor hands. He, therefore, had to crawl from where he was for nearly 3 hours to exit the building. Eventually, he caught a glimpse of the American tanks. Their captors had fled, and they were, therefore, liberated.

At last, facilities to help survivors were put up. Those who were sick were treated. Food was provided to all the survivors on an hourly basis for them to recover.

His weight was a measly forty pounds at the end, and he was nearly dying. It took up to six weeks for him to stabilize and be able to walk once again.

Chapter 6: The Story of Josef Salomonovic

Josef Salomonovic was born in 1938. His mother was known as Dora Salomonovoc, who hailed from Mahrisch-Ostrau, now currently known as Ostrava in the Czech Republic. She was a native German, but raised as Czech Jew. She attended a trade school where she met Josef's father, Erich, and got married and gave birth to Josef and his brother, Michal.

After the war and the cruel experience in the hands of the Nazis, Josef's mother, Josef, and his elder brother went back to Ostrava. It was there where he resumed a normal lifestyle and was able to enjoy games, such as football, after a gruesome period. His teeth developed within a short period, but could not quickly shed off some of the learned behaviors, such as hiding a piece of bread during his time of survival. He continues to make jokes that he still devours his meals while standing when alone, since no one was permitted to relax during the forced march.

After completing his education levels, he pursued mechanical engineering at university, then did compulsory military service, and lastly, went back to his mother. She worked in a particular power plant, and was a member of a specific gymnastics club, which endeared her to a lot of friends. She spotted a copper bracelet made by her late husband before the eruption of the war. It had been well-maintained by her Aunt Berta, who also had sent some food to Josef while he was at the camp.

In the 30s, Josef found the woman of his life. Her name was Elisabeth, and she came from Vienna. This took her mother by surprise, such that, when he divulged to her his plans of marrying her, she wanted to commit suicide. For instance, she headed straight to the kitchen and started putting her head on fire. Luckily, Josef saved her before any harm had been done. Later on, Josef married the love of his life and migrated to Vienna, where he got a job in the engineering field, where he had studied. During his mother's last moments on Earth, she became blind, so she went to live in a home care center. All that she had wished for Joseph and her brother had come to pass. For instance, they now had plenty of food to sustain them; they had proper bedding, and they were no longer subjected to cruel beatings. On her last day with him, they had walked together a few steps within the home care compound while being supported by him. She died in 1992, aged 88 years. His elder brother, Michal, also stayed in Ostrava. Of the thousands of Jews who were on board that train that took them to the ghetto, only forty-six of them managed to survive the Holocaust. Currently, three of them are alive, and they are Josef and Michal Salomonovic, together with a woman living in Munich. Josef has a grown-up daughter whom he named Katya, after the guard who had saved his life while at the camp.

His Ordeal

At the age of three, Josef remembered his mother telling him that, as a family, they were going to tour Poland. This was in 1941, after the occupation of Moravia and Bohemia by the Germans. Those occupying the place where they were headed had instructed their parents to go to the bunny railway station in Prague. Before receiving those instructions, his family had sought permission to travel to Shangai, but the Germans had ignored their request for no apparent reason. Apparently, his mother didn't know what was going on at that time. Therefore, they continued with their plans of making a trip to Poland. On their travel date, Joseph put on two shirts, alongside a coat and sweater. He also carried along his chamber pot, which he put inside a bag. After meticulously planning, his mother came up with a list of items she considered vital during their journey, which included things such as a filter to use in skimming milk, among others. Little did she know that milk was going to be a hard-to-reach commodity.

They boarded a train majorly composed of Jew-speaking people and were headed to the Lodz ghetto, a place explicitly reserved for the Jews. The family of four was forced to sleep on the same bed. His mother was forced to work in a paper factory, while his father was enrolled in a German metal factory. All this while, little Josef had to spend an entire day by himself while his elder brother was forced to spend his time straightening up bent needles at his place of work. Many of those who lived in the ghetto died due to the terrible weather conditions, and diseases such as typhoid fever. Others succumbed to the beatings unleashed to them by their masters, while others died of hunger. Those who found themselves in this place hardly had enough food for themselves, which made them severely malnourished and weak. For instance, when Josef's baby teeth came out, nothing replaced them, due to the lack of nutrition to enable growth of new teeth. It reached a point where his father had to trade his precious watch for a block of bread. He got accustomed to this environment, and it was all that he could call home. He had his family around and loved them, but was not aware of the single word that sent chills of fear down the spines of the other people around them. "Sperre" was the word.

During such rounds, known as "Sperre Jews", those residing within a particular building were rounded up, and those regarded as parasites due to their inability to work due to various conditions, such as typhoid fever, the old people and the children were taken away to be killed. In one instance, he remembered his father hiding in the roof of their apartment after learning an impending Sperre. Many of the children were collected from their hiding place and taken for a killing mission. Somewhere in 1944, they were, again, forced to move from the ghetto to Auschwitz. His parents had to backpack their belongings, and after a short journey, they arrived at their destination. Upon arrival, they were welcomed by a group that consisted of thin men wearing striped clothing and were banging on their cattle car and urging them to step out of the way. They were without any of their belongings. Then the men were told to go the right, while the women were to go the left. His father took his elder brother's hand, bent down, then mumbled something to him and finally kissed him. In an instant, he left, never to be seen again by Josef.

On the other hand, Josef was taken to another building by his mother. When they reached the building, they were required to strip off their clothes. He looked around but couldn't catch a glimpse of any other children within the vicinity. All he could see were women being shaved; others being beaten, and yet others yelling and sobbing. At this juncture, he let go off his mother's hand and wandered off into the sea of people, thereby losing contact with his mother. It was at this point in the process when he came into contact with a guard working for the SS, commonly known as "Kapos". Josef gave a long look at her features as she guided him by her hand, taking him back to the mount of clothes. The guard instructed him to take his things. While at it, he managed to recover his coat and white shoes with laces. The steel spoon he had in the jacket was still intact, and it saved his life. After he finished dressing up, the guard hugged him, then put a piece of chocolate in his mouth, then led him out of the room. Out there, they saw women who were trembling as they waited in a line. His shoelaces were undone, since his mother had always taken care of them.

They had reached the point where the guards who were manning the place directed some of the children to the gallows while providing chocolates to others. What also surprised him was the music that was being played in the vicinity, the two turtles found at the place, the doctor with an eye collection, and the river that was occasionally black.

He was then directed to the section of the barracks that comprised of naked women. His efforts to locate the whereabouts of his mother were still futile. Due to their shaven nature, all the women there resembled one another. It was only after his mother came forward and started tying his shoelaces that he was able to identify her. She took him and they were able to travel together during their work trips in the various destinations. The Germans referred to such arrangements as "closed transport". After a few days at the camp, they were designated to head to the Stutth camp that was also home to his elder brother and father. Nights at the camps were hell for Joseph, as the mornings grew colder. He shivered a lot during the morning parade, where the slaves were counted. He always resorted to standing between the legs of his mother to get some warmth, and even wondered why his life was spared, yet many children were executed at the camps.

Later on, her mother found out that his father had been murdered using a lethal phenol injection to his heart. At this juncture, she made a request that was rarely heard of or even tried by other prisoners.She requested a guard to bring her eldest son to him so that he can hand over his socks to young Josef, who was severely affected by the cold weather. It was ultimately a big request at a place where a mere stare at a guard could lead to severe beatings that could lead to death. According to Josef, she was a brave woman. Eventually, her request was granted, and Michal was brought to her. They finally talked about the death of their father. On a lighter note, she was subjected to a lighter punishment of knee bends after she openly asked the guard a question regarding the socks she had asked for—something which was strictly prohibited and could earn somebody a hefty punishment.

During the nights, his mother snuck him to the guard's bathroom to draw out the water from the bowl using her hands, then gave it to young Josef to drink. Although it was considered as something risky to undertake, she knew that any inmate who followed all the instructions to the letter would eventually die, because the main reason for the rules was to accomplish the mission of killing the Jews through starvation and dehydration. In November that year, his mother and brother were dispatched to Dresden, which was a bullet assembly factory. Josef was left behind. However, his mother, Diana, was able to convince the guards operating his camp to leave him alone and accept his presence. She also sought the services of another prisoner who was of Dutch origin to craft a letter to his Aunt known as Berta, and who stayed in Mahren to borrow food. It was through such engagements that Josef was awoken one day at night by his mother and provided with a slice of bread that was handsomely covered in butter and some sugar sprinkles, which was a rare delicacy that could be found in such a facility at such a time. Eventually, he was transferred to the Dresden factory where his mother labored. Within the first few weeks of his stay there, an inspection of the slaves by the SS got underway. Josef took cover inside a laundry basket to avoid discovery. However, he was noticed by one of the Nazis who had opened the basket and ordered that he should be killed the following day. That was on the 13th of February 1945, on a clear night sky.

Unknown to the Germans, the allied bombers stealthily arrived in the darkness. Together with his mother, they were able to hide in the basement area of the factory. He also vividly remembered being instructed by one of the Germans to open his mouth whenever a bomb went off. It rained bombs for the next two days, and all they could do was just to watch the glasses of the building being flung apart. Luckily for them, they were able to survive the onslaught, and came out unscathed. All this time, he was pressed to his mother. The scene outside the factory depicted several deaths of the Germans on the street. While on the streets, his shoes got stuck on the molten tarmac road. He was taken aback, looking at how well-fed the corpses were, in deep contrast to their health.

His mother provided him with some pieces of sugar to eat in case she would not make it back from the cleanup exercises she was forced to undertake. Due to the hunger pangs that he was feeling, he could not help rubbing at the matchbox containing the sugar all day long until it faded, as he waited for his mother to come back from the cleaning. He imagined how sweet it would be. Luckily, she made it through the day, and in the evening, she was able to share the sugar. After this event, they were continuously shifted within the various camps, and back to where they were at the factory. As a way to enable him to survive, his mother taught him how to use a spoon to rasp a raw potato so that he could eat it, since he hadn't grown any other teeth due to malnutrition at the ghetto camp.

At the start of the winter, Josef developed another significant challenge: His body began developing cysts as huge as strawberries. They were so painful to him, especially when he laid down. Besides that, they were full of pus and blood. Due to a lack of bedding for the slaves, the cysts busted and got smeared on the wooden floor. His mother offered him her stomach to lie on. She continuously offered him encouragement, and how they would, one day, overcome such conditions and be able to get themselves amenities, such as a mattress to sleep on, and escape the current sufferings forever. During one of the winter nights, Josef could no longer control the pain due to the bleeding cysts. Some of the prisoners suggested that he leave the place; yet it was winter outside. To contain all that noise, they took him outside, ripped off some parts of her shirt and used them to tie up the open cysts, wrapped him inside a blanket, then placed him inside a crate full of shavings. He remembered praying to G-d that night to take away his life, since he could no longer continue to sustain the pain he was undergoing. When morning came, his mother, together with other slaves, emerged from the barracks, and life had to go on. With an escort of several SS personnel, a cart, and two horses, they headed in the southern direction. Very often, a number of slaves could collapse due to extreme fatigue. He also became overwhelmed with this particular journey due to the wounds he had on his body. He said to his mother that he could no longer continue with the journey. She, therefore, carried him along. When she was also too tired to continue carrying him, she went up close to the master's cart and placed Josef somewhere on the back side where he could not be seen, and she also prayed that none of the Germans turned around to see what she was doing.

After walking for a considerable distance, all of a sudden, they heard the sound of an aircraft bomber. They were ordered to scamper to the trenches around the road. Her mother covered him and his brother using a blanket, and instructed them not to stand up or utter any word. The other slaves with the Germans continued with their journey, leaving behind Josef, his mother, and brother. After a while, they got up and scampered into a nearby forest. While crossing a particular section of the forest, they were able to catch a glimpse of a man donning a railway uniform. His mother begged the man to help them. Upon seeing how wasted and thin they were, he took them to a nearby farmhouse and concealed them inside a barn. He later brought them some food, which consisted of milk and bread. Josef was utterly amazed by how soothing and sweet the milk tasted. The man later opened the barn after three nights and announced to them that the Americans were around, which meant that they had been liberated from the Germans. Josef then found his way to a pond at the center of the village, where he met an American soldier who gifted him with a toy plane and told him to stay with it.

Chapter 7: The Story of Ruchama Rachel Rothstein (Rachel Roth)

Rachel Roth was born in the year 1926 in Warsaw, Poland. She was a daughter to Mr. Samuel Rothstein and Mrs. Golda. Her siblings included three other girls, namely: Reginka, Justinka, and Davidik. She lived a normal childhood life that was filled with love and a religious background in the Jewish faith. She appreciated life when young, so she made a lot of friends, played with the family, and did all the things that made her happy and contented. Some of her hobbies included going to the beach, appreciating nature by walking around her neighborhood, and reading books and novels that were available to her. Things started to take an ugly twist with the growth of the Nazis and their ideology. By the time she was thirteen years of age, the Germans had attacked her land and defeated their army, which led to the capture of their capital city, Poland. This event gave the Germans a reason for hatching a plan to wipe out the entire Jewish population found within the captured grounds, and any other place within their territory. The Germans had an extreme hatred for the Jews, and utilized any extreme measures to ensure that they be completely wiped out.

It was such a turn of events that took away her sense of being human, including her freedom. After the invasion, her motherland was divided into several zones—of which, one was turned to a holding place for the Jew population, including her family, and was referred to as the "ghetto". The place was so appalling, with a lack of the necessary amenities, such as food and clothing, among other basic human needs. These led to starvation and the spread of a lot of diseases caused by poor sanitation, overcrowding and starvation. It was such conditions that led to the death of her mother while in the ghetto. As such, she joined the others in the ghetto uprising and provided her support through smuggling weapons. This kind of reaction only compounded their troubles as the Nazis decided to reshuffle their living arrangements.

During this move, together with her grandfather and aunt, they were transferred to a place known as "Majdelk" by train, and forced to labor under harsh conditions. Later, Rachel and her Aunt Hela were moved to the Auschwitz concentration camp, where they spent two years. During specific periods at the camp, Rachel wanted to surrender to fate. However, she put in all she had to persevere up to the end of the ordeal. At the tail end of the war, they were moved to another location known as "Bergen-Belsen", where they were saved from the wrath of the Germans by the British in April 1945. Like the rest of the survivors, her story is also filled with sad stories of what went around the concentration camp, and the difficulties she had to endure to live another day. She also brought to the forefront her will to survive through the killings that surrounded her, and her hope of being rescued on one of the fine days. After being let free from that, she later got married and gave birth to five children. Currently, she stays in New York, and is a happy grandmother to her grandchildren. She shares her stories of the events in schools and other avenues to make sure that an event of such magnitude will never be repeated again. Her message to all is that nobody should ever let a Holocaust occur again.

Her Ordeal

It was in the year 1940, when the ugly head of Nazi segregation started to show up. This was after the defeat of the Warsaw army that saw the capture of Poland by the Germans. Eventually, they divided it into several zones. Her entire family was sent to a specific zone known as the "Warsaw Ghetto", which was reserved for the Jewish community. The main idea behind creating such a zone was to stuff all the Jew population into one common area, so that controlling them would become easier for the Germans. As such, life at the ghetto was extremely harsh and cruel. Thousands of Jews were swamped in from all over with no extra resources for them. As such, a lot of violence was witnessed at this place. Families such as Rachel's languished in utter poverty and lacked the essentials to sustain them. Due to the lack of enough food for the whole population living in this place, many of them became victims of mass starvation, leading to the death of many. As a result, many children were stripped off their innocence and took up the adult role of providing food to avert starvation. Children as young as Rachel had to step up to take the responsibilities of becoming the breadwinners of their families. The need to look for food made the children carefree, as they went on the search for food to feed their families. Some of them took great measures, such as sneaking around walls, to steal food to prevent their families from succumbing to starvation. Apart from this, the lack of the necessary sanitary essentials, such as water, restrooms, and the closeness of their houses, led to the spread of infectious and painful conditions that caused death among them.

According to her, it was a ghastly sight to behold. Poor health, extreme poverty, and hunger were so evident. Gangs of thin and pale people could be seen wandering without reason through the overcrowded streets. One could easily spot beggars along the walls of the buildings on the brink of death. Others would be seen collapsing from the effects of starvation. Every day, thousands of abandoned newborns were registered at the refugee camp. Death and spread of infectious diseases, such as tuberculosis, was a common thing. To bring it closer, her grandfather succumbed to typhoid while her brother's life was on the line after a typhoid breakout. In the ghetto, no form of institutions or schools was allowed. Nevertheless, such restrictions did not stop the likes of Rachel, among other young Jews, from trying to seek out opportunities to get an education. It was with great zeal and determination of a few that led to the establishment of a secret learning institution. As such, Rachel became one of the most dedicated who attended the school without fail. On the other hand, her teacher was also daring and dedicated to her work and, therefore, continued her classes with those children who were very eager to continue learning. Rachel developed a deep love for the chemistry lessons, but all this was eventually cut short with the start of deportations to the concentration camps.

As life continued to deteriorate in the ghetto, people there started to rise in arms concerning the kind of life that they lived. These forced the Nazis to start targeting the Jews to deport them to the death camps. They would perform violent raids at the ghetto that lead to the tearing apart of families, and sent the captured to these camps. Many families, including Rachel's, lived in the utmost fear during the raids. As such, Rachel's family built a secret bunker in their house in the hopes that it could protect them from the constant raids, and to continue to stay together. But things did not go according to plan. They needed to come out of the bunker to go and fend for the family; otherwise, they could starve to death. They had to go and hassle in the ghetto to acquire food. It was during such endeavors that some of Rachel's family members went out, never to return. It is believed that they were captured by the Nazis and sent out to the various deportation camps. Some of her family members who went out and never returned included her two sisters, mother, and brother. They were captured and sent to the camps. On the other hand, Rachel succeeded in evading the raids for some more time and lasted up to the time that the Warsaw Ghetto uprising started. Due to her deep hatred for the Nazis, she wholly participated in it. She smuggled weapons into her hood to enable the resistors to fight the Germans. As the resistance continued to take shape, the Germans discovered that some of the Jews were hiding in bunkers; therefore, to smoke them out, they set the bunkers on fire. These forced Rachel and her ilk to come out into the streets, which lead to a major confrontation between the two sides. Unluckily for them, they were eventually overpowered, and their members were sent to various concentration camps. As a result, Rachel and her aunt Hela found their fate leading them to one such camp.

This kind of resistance and another planned attack on the Germans made them get rid of the ghetto. Therefore, the remaining population was herded on to cattle carts and trains, then sent to Majdanek. Among those deported was Rachel Roth. She vividly remembered how she was holding on to her aunts' and grandfather's hand to avoid being separated from them. However, they were shoved and brutally kicked around. While raising their hands up in the air, they were forced to board the waiting carts while riffles were being pointed at them, ready to snuff out the life from anyone who dared to resist. At this moment, she and the rest of the people were so fearful of what was going to happen to them, let alone the matter of being separated from their family members who matter a lot to them. She described the train as it moved in a slow and rhythmic movement, as a great torment to her. She could register the boring click-clack sounds of the train's wheel on the rail, and how it suddenly gained speed toward their destiny. Such jarring causes the sea of humanity in the train to fall onto each other. Others collapsed due to overcrowding and heat on the train. This explained a lot how inhuman the Nazis were, and how being under the mercy of a fellow human could end up. Their first camp to be taken with her aunt Hela was Majdanek located in Lublin, Poland. Upon arrival, they were stripped naked, then provided with prison uniforms. Many of those who were taken to Majdanek were subjected to forced labor. The main cause of their death was harsh living conditions that did not allow them to live. Alternatively, those who appeared weak and could no longer work were taken to the gas chambers. Others died of hunger, communicable and stubborn diseases, shooting sprees, and overworking. To keep away the thoughts of hunger and other weird things that were happening in her mind, Rachel developed the tactic of telling stories. She narrated stories regarding the excellent Jewish dishes she had back then. By the use of imagery in her stories, she was able to captivate all their senses, which distracted them from what was happening around them. It was such kind of zeal and tuck exhibited by her despite her frail and fragile body that made one of the older prisoners encourage her to continue fighting until the end so that she could tell the world what the beasts had done to them. The older woman believed that Rachel had the capacity and will to go through whatever was happening around them. Through the use of stories, she was also able to keep the women entertained with Jewish traditions. As a result, she made the last days of an older woman wonderful instead of depressing. Watching the woman bearing a tired and sad look in her eyes, Rachel promised to fulfill what she had advised her. It was during that particular moment when she swore never to die, and that she would survive the whole ordeal, then go out there and tell the whole world about the stories of those who did not survive through it all.

On the day before her transfer to the Auschwitz camp, she and other women were taken to the gas chambers and told to wait there for transport to another camp, which was utterly deceptive. But by sheer luck, there was an accounting error that provided her with another shot at life. According to her, a small fraction of a second might appear useless in human life, but at other times, it could make a difference in situations about life and death. However, her grandfather was not spared. He was gassed at the time when the male prisoners were separated from the female ones in what the Nazis referred to as the "ultimate solution", just like the other prisoners.

The arrival at the Auschwitz-Birkenau was eerily the same. They either arrived on an overcrowded train or in cattle cars. That stopped immediately at the entry gate of the camp. The first common feature is the gate with German words on it. The same events happened to Rachel. They came out of their wagons and headed straight to form a row for the processing to start. After the selection process, they were rushed into a room where barbers awaited them. With no time at all, her hair was off her head. The barber used tailor scissors to perform that. Her hair was then mixed with the others from the different people, then put inside huge sacks by the other slaves. According to her, this was the way the Germans used to dehumanize the Jew population, because it was their symbol. Also, it is a method of creating a feeling of worthlessness within the Jew slaves who arrived at this place. They were then provided with what was referred to us the "hygienic bath". This comprised of cold streams of water emanating from showers. Rachel utilized this chance to satisfy her thirst for water after a horrendous journey on the cattle carts. But due to the fear that they were providing the slaves with unnecessary niceties, they quickly turned on the hot water system. After getting their bodies washed, the slaves were then scrambled into another room while naked and trembling from the ensuing cold as they waited to be provided with new attires. Women were provided with work dresses and loosely-fitting work shoes, and, in other instances, clogs.

On the other hand, the men had to contend with jackets and striped pants that had seen better days. These were the only clothes that were in their possession; therefore, they had to work and sleep in them. After being provided with the working attires, it was time for each slave to be given identification by inscribing a number on their arms. These meant that families and friends had to separate, which depended on the first initial of their last name. As such, Rachel went in different ways with her aunt. Upon reaching her destination, she encountered a prisoner wearing a white-and-blue striped dress, seated behind a table. She noted down her last and first names together with her place of birth. She then moved to the next table where a girl holding a device similar to a syringe waited for her. She then made some holes in her skin and injected some few ink drops on the bleeding patterns. After a few moments, she got her new identification. Her prison number was 48915. It got tattooed on her arm, together with a small triangle. Then, beneath the number was the half Star of David, which indicated that she was a Jew. These meant that her individuality was now taken, and she was now a mere property. Providing the Jews with unique numbers enabled the Nazis to track down the slaves easily, and also to deny them their means of living and identification. Such processes took dehumanization a notch higher, since they were regarded as numbers and not human beings. These numbers were their main source of identification in the facility.

At the camp, the routines, such as labor, were another form of genocide, referred to by the Germans as "extermination through work". Individuals who did not go straight to the gas chambers headed for work that stripped off any humanity in them that lead to their subsequent death. The living conditions at the camp were hell. Slaves were held up in old buildings that had no windows to let in air and light, and they were also not well-built to prevent any heat transfer, thus conducting heat and cold easily. The slaves used a bucket as their restroom. Also, there were no beds for prisoners; consequently, they had to contend with sleeping on the wooden planks.

On top of that, they were of a small size, roughly measuring 36 by 11 by 6 meters, with only two ventilators and a single door on each side. What appalled her were the living conditions and the number of inmates assigned to such a building. For instance, there were up to 500 prisoners living in the houses at any given time during her stay at the camp. She described the structure as one which was almost totally dark inside, with lousy smells emanating from mildew growing from the floor. In the building, there were several dark corridors. On each side, there were cement bunks that were divided using bricks. In each cubicle, up to ten girls fitted. They were then provided with black blankets that looked and smelled suspicious, before switching off the lights. They were so squeezed-together that they had to lie on one another to fit. At the camp, a slave was identified by the color of the triangle ingrained on their uniform. For instance, yellow for the Jew, green for a criminal, and red for a political prisoner, and so on. She and her aunt Hela were assigned the task of breaking stones. Other prisoners got easy jobs that made others feel envious. Her workday came to a halt when the SS-in-charge signaled through a whistle, which was usually in the evenings as the sun was going down. Many of them were overly exhausted, such that they had to drag themselves back to the camp due to hunger and exhaustion.

Hunger was the main thing that preoccupied the minds of the prisoners all the time. Also, water was an issue at the camp. The water there was filled with dirt, which made most of the women suffer a lot at the camp. Due to the lack of clean water and scarce food, people were easily infected with contagious and infectious diseases. For instance, diarrhea was a common thing among the slaves. Also, there was an outbreak of scabies during her time there, which led to the gassing of many prisoners in the pretext of controlling the disease. The disease caused itchy sores on the skin of an individual, and a scratch on them led to their eventual spread on the body. Rachel feared to be infected, as it would send her to the gas chambers. During her work, an abscess formed below her arm, which could render her as a worker who could not work, and a candidate to be sent to the gas chambers. At the camp, the prisoners kept tracking the seasons and time to pass the time. Rachel concentrated on identifying the different types of seasons while in the camp, which she used to remember the significant events that happened at the camp. As such, she remembered a particular session when she was recalled from her field and assigned the work of a *bekleidungskammer*. Her job was to go through women's inner clothing and make bundles out of them. Things of good value were taken to Germany to be used there. In the summer of 1944, things started showing some signs of freedom. Transport into the camp became less—selections at the gate stop. The crematorium was shut down. There was a rumor of Russians defeating the Germans and also being bombarded by the allies. Those at the ovens were starting to dismantle the crematorium, which gave Rachel a hope of seeing the day after. They were then moved to the Bergen-Belsen camp, where the British army liberated them.

Part III: Liberation from the Nazis

Chapter 8: The End of the Nazi Rule

The effects of World War II were devastating. The scars were spread all over Europe and other parts of the world to date. It was a war that left 60 million people as refugees, much of Europe destroyed, millions of homes and businesses destroyed, and up to 20 million people dead in Europe alone.

In the Hitler extermination camps, more than 11 million people met their deaths because the Nazis saw their religion, sex, race, physical, or mental ability as lesser. Of the 11 million, 6 million were Jews. A good number of those who found it in themselves to resist the Nazi system were put under the same category of those to be exterminated. The German soldiers who died in the war were estimated to have reached 5.3 million. Indeed, World War II was, by far, the most destructive war in recorded history.

The devastation was all over. Even the Nazi's well-organized system was at a mess when the war came to an end. This is best described by the way the German Nazi leaders tried to close the Auschwitz concentration camp and starting the "death march" of the Jews to Germany.

The Defeat of Germany

In mid-1945, the Germans started experiencing internal strife. Himmler and Goering began to withdraw from the leadership of Hitler. The two started planning their rise to power. The formal surrender of Germany in the Second World War happened a week after the death of Hitler (through suicide). In his last will, Hitler observed that the fall and defeat of Germany rest entirely on the shoulders of the "International Jewry and its helpers." He urged the Germans to adhere to the "the strict observance of the racial laws and with merciless resistance against the universal prisoners of all peoples," which pertains to the Jews. The will was read in a German bunker on April 29, 1945.

Following the eventual defeat of Germany in the Second World War, its troops evacuated the concentration camps, sending convicts away from the advancing enemies. Termed the "death marches," the process continued until Germany surrendered officially in 1945. The walk resulted in the death of close to four hundred thousand people.

The allies had foreseen the collapse of the Nazis. As early as 1943, the allies had started convening conferences to discuss possible future legal actions to be met against the German war criminals. Soon after the collapse of the Nazi government, Germany was divided into four allied-controlled zones. Authority over the country was placed in the hands of the Allied Control Commission, which had representatives from France, Britain, the United States, and the Soviet Union.

The surrender of the Nazis meant that the first people to be liberated were those in the concentration camps. It was in those concentration camps that the world finally came to understand the full extent of the savageness of Hitler's regime. Corpses were littered everywhere. Severely malnourished victims were found in the camps.
In fact, due to starvation, forced labor, and hunger over the years, most of those in the concentration camps were just skin and bones, and many died soon after.
Because of the starvation they were subjected to, many of the recently-released prisoners had reached a point where they could not digest food. The food offered to the emaciated prisoners by liberators did not help, as half of them died within a few days after being rescued. This was evidenced in Auschwitz and other camps. For those liberated prisoners who were lucky enough to get nutritionally-dense concoctions made by medical staff, health was regained, and survival was assured.

One can only imagine the state the prisoners were in when they were released from the concentration camps. They were suffering from starvation. Many were in a truly filthy state and were suffering from vulnerable diseases. Because of the unhygienic condition, the camps hosted infections such as typhus, which started and spread through the camps easily. In Bergen-Belson, for example, out of a population of 50,000 survivors, 13,000 died soon after being liberated. This was despite a lot of effort being put by doctors to treat and contain the diseases—a majority of them having been caused by typhus.

Tremendous efforts were made to contain the epidemics. Bodies of survivors were taken through rigorous disinfecting procedures. Their possessions were disinfected, too. Thousands of corpses found at the camps by liberators and those of prisoners who died at their watch were disposed of. In some instances, like in Bergen-Belson, a whole camp was burned to the ground to prevent the spread of an epidemic. This was the reason Bergen-Belson was never used as a memorial to the dead, unlike Auschwitz.

Trials and the Continued Fight for Justice

There were 12 other trials conducted after the Nuremberg trial, and which were done under the auspices of IMT. These were, however, done before the United States military tribunals. Even those Germans accused of perpetrating crimes in these zones were tried using the same manner. Many of the defendants in these trials were the guard units and staff at concentration camps, and those accused of committing crimes against Allied military and civilians.

German leaders who committed crimes in certain countries or territories were generally caught and returned to those specific countries where the crimes were committed. The best example of such an arrest and trial was that of Rudolf Walter Richard Hess in 1947, which was conducted in Kracow, Poland. Hess was the commandant of the Auschwitz concentration camp.

In countries such as Poland, Hungary, Bulgaria, Romania, Yugoslavian, and the Soviet Union, many trials of German collaborators and war criminals were conducted soon after the war until the early 1950s.

The number of Nazi officials involved in one way or another in the systematic displacement, murder, or committing of a war crime was big. Many war criminals were never arrested nor brought to trial to be punished. At some point, the FRG tried to set up an agency for crime investigation. This was to help in streamlining the investigation of the offenders. These efforts led to some well-documented trials, like the trial of the Auschwitz personnel, which was later conducted. In the end, only about 20% of the 150,000 Nazi war criminals were ever tried. Today, the search continues for the Holocaust criminals and Nazi collaborators.

How the Nazi Leaders Tried to Cover Up Their Crimes

There were around 42,000 concentration camps set up by the Nazi government. These offered a perfect way through which Hitler and the Nazi leadership could perfect their crimes against the Jews and other minorities. Auschwitz was the biggest camp, where the Nazis gassed an average of 6,000 people each day. In total, more than 1.1 million people met their deaths here.

In Auschwitz, it was the advancing Soviet army that posed a threat to the Nazis. Some of the marches were long, some of them even hundreds of miles. According to the survivors of these death marches, anyone who looked weak would be shot on the spot. Even bending over to tighten a shoelace would attract a Nazi bullet.

Toward the end of 1944, the allied forces had taken over most of Nazi-controlled Europe. The Nazis had to think of a way to escape, or create a better endgame for themselves.

Despite the Nazis' best efforts, the ruins remained, with the evidence of what they had been doing in the camp since 1940.

While the Nazis called the marches an evacuation, it was clear that the intention was to send prisoners to Germany to work as laborers. Many of the prisoners were asked to get into trains; others were killed as they tried to escape. And still, some managed to run and escape into sub-zero temperatures.

About 7,000 prisoners who were considered weak and unfit to work were left at the camp. This was not enough for the SS command, though. An order came down, instructing the SS soldiers to kill all the remaining prisoners. Even though more than 700 of the prisoners were murdered, order at the camp started breaking down, and this saw some SS officers starting to escape, themselves. The remaining SS officers tried to burn documents to hide the Nazi crimes.

Of the remaining 7,000 prisoners at the camp, half of them died soon after being liberated by the Red Army. This was caused by exhaustion, starvation, and disease. The others recovered slowly, and began their lives as displaced persons.

A few people were able to grasp the magnitude of the horrors meted on the people at the concentration camps. Even leading newspapers like *The New York Times* only mentioned the city where Auschwitz was located. Nothing was said about Auschwitz and the horrific scenes and stories from the camp. A horrifying scene beyond description met the Soviet army that arrived at the camp on the 27th of January 1945.

In their hurry to destroy everything and escape before the Red Army arrived, the Nazi soldiers forgot to destroy one of the stores. In the store, the Red Army discovered prisoners' items which the Nazis would have transported back to the Reich.

What Options Did The Survivors Have?

As you would expect, the millions of prisoners liberated from the concentration camps would have wanted to return to their homes. But this war was unlike any other. Several factors prevented many of the displaced and the newly released prisoners from returning to their original homes. Many of these people, especially the prisoners, could not return to their homes because their homeland is what they now call "cursed soil."

Chances were that a survivor couldn't return to their home because it was destroyed, or because they were the only surviving family members. Many of the survivors didn't even have hope of finding a long-lost friend or a family member. The situation was made even worse by the fact that most of the European societies at the time, where the concentration camp survivors came from, were rife with anti-Semitism. This meant that going back home would be suicidal, or they would be very unwelcome at best. This drove many of the survivors to want to leave Europe and start a new life elsewhere.

Some Continued to Be Kept in Concentration Camps

The physical conditions of the survivors was bad. The health conditions were terrible, and there was a huge risk that typhus could break out. This led to the allied forces retaining the survivors in the concentration camps, at least until the epidemic risks were put under control.

In Dachau, for example, when the U.S. soldiers arrived on April 12, 1945, they found thousands upon thousands of corpses of emaciated bodies piled inside boxcars. They found a recently-used gas chamber filled with excrement and human brains splattered on the floors. They also found a few victims who were still alive, but who were horribly weak.

It is worth noting that, at a time after the German commanders abandoned the camps and the liberating soldiers arrived, German soldiers who had been left to guard the prisoners met their deaths. The camp was in a most horrifying state to the newly-arrived allied soldiers. They found a few combative and resistant German soldiers. Having taken stock of what they saw, the American soldiers rounded up the German soldiers and executed them on the spot.

In some instances, it was reported that prisoners caught their former captors and beat them to death. In the Dachau concentration camp alone, at least 50 German soldiers died on that day.

Some Committed Suicide

After being released, many Holocaust prisoners committed suicide. Many theories have been floating as to the real reasons behind these suicides. However, some of the logical reasons include the traumatic nature of their experience. The other reason that many survivors committed suicide was that they were very ill physically, they were grieving for their murdered families, or they were still living in dehumanizing conditions. Instead, they aspired to successfully cement to the world their discontinuity. These words are likely to be based more on the stigma associated with suicide rather than any study.

Moving to Palestine and Other Parts of the World

The allies had a tough time deciding what to do with the liberated survivors who could not re-join their old communities. In a nutshell, the four occupying allies, namely, the USA, Britain, France, and USSR, dragged their feet at helping to relocate the millions of displaced people.

Hundreds of thousands of displaced Jewish persons who were unwilling to go back to Eastern Europe because of anti-Semitism were put in camps. Soon after, these displaced persons were joined by thousands of refugees who were migrating from several liberation points.

The U.S. government still had very restrictive immigration laws at the time. For the many displaced Jewish persons who wished to go to the U.S., they found out that they were not welcome. Even though MS St. Louis, which had carried at least 900 Jews, was refused to dock in the U.S. in 1939, it showed just how tough it was to enter the country after the war, even when the reasons were obvious. The captain of the ship steered the ship back to Europe. This was a definite death sentence to those trying to escape the solid grip of the Nazis, which was all over Europe.

The United States eventually took in more than 400,000 displaced persons. But during the most difficult time (the first year after liberation), only 16,000 got into the country. Hundreds of thousands of visa applicants were turned down.

Things were not good for the Jews who wanted to migrate to Palestine, either. Britain had a weak hand at the defunct League of Nations, which severely restricted the migration of Jews to Palestine. Britain feared to alienate the Arab residents of the region, and this meant that the British government was very harsh toward the Jewish displaced persons who wanted to sail and start living in Palestine. The British army intercepted many ships. In one case, in 1947, the British intercepted a ship that had 4,500 Holocaust survivors at the port of Haifa. They were forcibly returned to Germany.

In 1948, the Displaced Persons Act was initiated by the Congress. This Act covered about 500,000 displaced persons who needed to relocate to a different state. Over the years, that Act expired.With time, the Refugee Act replaced it.

The Creation of the State of Israel

After being released from concentration camps, survivors started organizing themselves politically. In Bergen-Belson, for example, a committee was formed in 1945, whose aim was to propagate a Zionist nation.

Palestine was a British colony, and the decision to carve out a Jewish state was made without the consultation of the Palestinian people. The creation of a new state meant that hundreds of thousands of Arab Palestinians were displaced. It is for this reason that Israel remains such a hotbed politically.

The Middle East has been embroiled in wars and territory fights ever since the state of Israel was created. On the one hand, the supporters of Israel believe that the Jewish people have suffered a lot, and they deserve to have a country that is free of anti-Semitism. On the other hand, those who support the Palestinians say that, even though the Jewish people deserve a place to call home, it shouldn't be at the expense of the Arab-Palestinians.

The Long-Term Effects of the Holocaust

The result of the said Holocaust has continued to affect more people across the world. After the disaster, the survivors found it difficult to go back home due to the extent of their displacement. Most people lost their families, dignity, and even their lives in the process. For the survivors, the Holocaust remains a bitter part of their memories as they share their stories across the world. Over the epochs that followed, regular Germans have had to live with the angry legacy of the Holocaust. The survivors and the families of the victims have sought after reimbursement of fortune and possessions seized during the Nazi eons. Since 1953, the Germany government has paid the surviving Jews and the Jewish people at large as a show of taking responsibility for the crimes committed against the Jews by German troops over the years.

Following efforts to work closely with the victims in assisting them to change their lives by recovering their health in different ways, most people came forward to assist.

The creation of Israel resulted from the pressure put on the allies to offer a dwelling place.

Chapter 9: The Holocaust Anniversaries

Besides Germany, many other states have marked, remembered, and honored the events. For instance, the United Kingdom observes the Holocaust Memorial Day annually on the twenty-seventh of January since 2001. The Holocaust Remembrance Day is also a recognized national event in Italy to commemorate the tragic loss of lives during the Holocaust that occurred during the Second World War. This phase of war consisted of a massive genocide that claimed the lives of about 17 million people, with thirty-five percent of the victims being Jews.

Up until now, there are more national days of remembrance that are being acknowledged after the 60/7 resolution that was made in 2005. The main objective of the then-adopted resolution was for the interest of the future generations, that they would be spared from acts of genocide. The Second World War broke out in September 1939. Germany, a member of the axis, invaded Poland. The invasion of Poland and the building of the Auschwitz camp were to imprison people of Polish origin. At least 1.3 million prisoners were sent in the short span of five years after its official opening. Both girls and boys faced sheer terror in the hands of their oppressors. Conviction into the Auschwitz death camp was an immediate contract into forced labor and extreme torture for daring to be an anti-Nazi. The inmates were subjected to brutal labor even in the scorching summer sun and the harsh winter weather conditions. The conditions in the Auschwitz camp wasn't favorable at all; in its peak, a bed would be shared by around five to ten inmates. The Nazi brutality removed all manner of decency and humanity. Despite the labor, sanitation wasn't at its best. Typhoid outbreaks were frequent, and the inmates who got infected by the disease would mercilessly get shot to death. The Nazis put up the Auschwitz camp to eliminate the Polish by labor, but the camp later turned into a Jewish genocide facility. People of more inferior identities such as artists, gypsies, the queer communities, and the handicapped (Roma and Sinti) were considered less important, and were eliminated. All sorts of prisoners were held in the uttermost brutal and inhuman conditions, such that a majority starved to death, were tortured, or died at the hands of their oppressors. Children were sadly not excluded from the horror. Infants and twins were subjected to inhumane medical experiments.

In mid-January 1945, the Soviets drew closer, forcing the Nazis to start implementing that the Auschwitz prisoners were to march. Any prisoner who fell was tagged as weak and was shot. More than fifteen thousand lives were lost during such kinds of marches.

Another factor would be anti-Semitism. Anti-Semitism is prejudice or hostility and discrimination against the Jews. Though very similar to racism, anti-Semitism is more brutal and had claimed many lives from the Jewish people. The Jewish people who were situated in other countries other than Poland, at the time, also experienced traces of anti-Semitism. Despite that, religious hatred and differences also cost the Jews their lives. Some people across the world couldn't even trade with them, let alone accept the Jewish people. A number of Jews were prosecuted for holding on to their religious beliefs. With Adolph Hitler's Nazi party politically leading the German troops, Jews were killed and eliminated in large numbers. This was broadly due to political differences and blind obedience to the Nazis. Adolph Hitler considered the Jews unsuitable for the German standards in terms of race. With a large sum of the power vested on Hitler as the German leader come, the Jews, mostly in German protectorates and colonies, fell vulnerable to any order against them from the German leaders. Other factors include political threats, coercion, xenophobia, and profiteering. Xenophobia against foreign Jews in any given country created hostility towards them. The cause of xenophobia was a fear of the country being overpowered by the Jews in their own country financially, politically, or even educationally. Anti-Semitism and xenophobia manifested and were evident in noticeable instances in history, i.e., the Rhineland massacre (Rhineland was German's military base, presumed to be an execution camp, too). Hatred and discrimination were evident in public, for instance, pogroms and killings by mobs, military raids to homes and villages of targeted people, and police attacks on civilians.

The war continued with the allies; France, Britain, America, and the Soviet Union fought against the axis, which consisted of Japan, Italy, and Germany (Rome-Berlin-Tokyo axis). The Second World War was started mainly because of the political takeover by Adolph Hitler and the Nazi party in 1933. Adolph set out aggressive foreign policies that poked the allies. This war started on the 1st of September 1939. In 1945, the Second World War concluded with an invasion of Germany by the Soviet Union and the allies after the invasion of Berlin by the Soviet troops. On this very occasion, the Nazi super leader, Adolph Hitler, died. The axis body surrendered to the allies' power on the 8th of May 1945. The allies accepted the German surrender a week after their leader, Adolph Hitler, allegedly committed suicide. After the war, members of Hitler's paramilitary organization, the Schutzstaffel (SS), as well as collaborationist members, stood under trial for committing war crimes.

The Holocaust ranged from 1933 to 1945, claimed the lives of 11 million people, six million being Jews, and 1.1 million being children. On the 27th of January that very same year, the German death camp based in Poland, Auschwitz, was liberated by the Soviets. Thousands and thousands of sick and dying prisoners were rescued, and a pile of victims' corpses was found in the camp's premises. This has left a sad, unfading scar in the hearts of the growing generations left by the torture the victims had to endure. Since 1996, the Holocaust Remembrance Day has been legally accorded as a nationwide anniversary in Germany. This is to honor and pay tribute to the befallen victims of the Holocaust phase. Military bodies and army generals were rendered without arms after the great liberation. Rhineland was taken from Germany's rule as an army base. Later in November 2005, the United Nations general assembly adopted a resolution, 60/7. It was put out by Israel as a way of marking the Holocaust anniversary annually. It spread a message of peace to the coming generations, who would look back at the events of the Auschwitz Holocaust to preach peace and stop acts of genocide in the coming future. For the past anniversaries, some countries use a symbolic special siren to alert its citizens of the Remembrance Day.

As soon as the siren goes off, people (including pedestrians and drivers) all come to a halt as a symbolic honor salute for the victims. The frequency of the international Holocaust anniversary is annually celebrated on the 27th of January. This is an honorable way of commemorating the tragedy that occurred during the Second World War, the offense of genocide that put to death six million Jews and eleven million more people by the military bodies and generals of the Nazi regime, and all its collaborators. The liberation of the Auschwitz Birkenau concentration camp and two other extermination camps by the red army in the last year of World War II is an important event in the world's chronological history. The first Holocaust Remembrance Day was marked and acknowledged in Israel, one and a half years after she gained her independence. This occasion was held on December 1949, where a burial ceremony was celebrated in Jerusalem to lay to rest thousands and thousands of bones of the Jews who had died in a concentration camp called Flossenbürg near Munich.

The Holocaust Remembrance Day was made official by the Jewish Law in Israel in the year 1959. All the annual Holocaust celebrations in Israel are to be attended by the president, the prime minister, and recognized dignities. Six significant torches are lit up to remember the occurrence of the World War and all the lives it claimed. Ever since, to honor these events, people all over the world light up candles and stay in a vigil in memory of the ones who died over the terror of the Holocaust. Israeli television and radio stations air the history and events of the period and the World War, and memories of survivors are also acknowledged. In Poland, hundreds of thousands of people take part in a national walk called "the march of the living," walking quietly in honor of the dead, starting from Auschwitz to Birkenau, marking the biggest Nazi concentration camp. Many people fly in from different countries all around the world for this event. On the 1st of March 1988, approximately three hundred thousand people attended Poland's annual walk in honor of the fallen victims. Though Israel and the United Nations have tried to raise a beacon to suppress any future trace and threat of genocide, anti-Semitic attacks and discrimination are, again, on the rise, and are becoming increasingly common throughout the world. A recent study shows that the attacks are both in public and private space. This makes the affected persons, in this case, the Jews, feel very insecure and unprotected, probably questioning their place in society. We need to come together as a united human race to kick out the alarming issue of genocide to prevent another horrifying event or threat of a rising Holocaust in the near future. This is entirely for the sake of the coming generations in the future to give them a better hope and a peaceful world. The next Holocaust Remembrance Day anniversary will be held next year, Monday, 27th January. Support the International Holocaust Remembrance Day for the gain and benefit of tomorrow's generation. Turn up and support it!

Chapter 10: The Holocaust Lies, Denials, Distortions, and Misconceptions

The Holocaust is part of history that no one can erase. But there is a lot of misconception, lies, denial, and distortion surrounding it. In the U.K., one in every 20 adults believes the Holocaust never took place, and 8% of them think it's a story blown out of proportion. The magnitude of the genocide doesn't seem real. This is according to one poll carried out during a Holocaust Memorial Day.

Those questioned cannot help wondering who counted the Jews who died during the massacre.

According to those who doubt the whole Holocaust, it is likely that two million people died. But history states that over six million Jews died in the genocide. This is a research carried out by Holocaust Memorial Day Trust, which was started in the U.K. by the government to support and promote remembrance of the Holocaust internationally. These findings are not different from what was found in the other seven European countries.

According to the poll, some people know nothing about the Holocaust; one in every three didn't say much or knew nothing at all. About 5% of those who participated in the poll had not heard of the Holocaust.

In France, among the people aged between 18 and 34 years, 20% knew nothing about the Holocaust. In Austria, 12% of the respondents from the same age bracket confessed of not ever hearing about the Holocaust. In the U.S., a survey revealed that 9% of young people, especially the millennials, could not remember hearing about the Holocaust. The number of people not caring about the Holocaust was shocking.

According to one member of the Holocaust Memorial Day Trust, Olivia Marks, these poll respondents cannot be classified as deniers.

It is ignorance, which makes them easy to believe distortions and myths. Most people who are middle-aged skipped this topic in their school curriculum, and it wasn't included, hence the reason their students have never heard of it.

One of the 93 children who escaped narrowly from the Theresienstadt camp, Steven Frank, says the figures are worrying. He just cannot understand why people are not bothered by what happened to millions of people during the massacre. He is dedicated to sharing about the Holocaust and will not stop even if he meets people who tell him that it did not happen. This is part of the world's past that should not be ignored, because people might relax, giving history a chance to repeat itself.

A positive thing about the poll was that 83% agreed it was important to raise awareness about the Holocaust, and 76% thought more has to be done to let people know about the genocide. Every year, the Holocaust Memorial is marked, but nothing much is discussed, except this extraordinary and unfortunate event that happened many years ago.

The same remembrance brings memories of the recent massacre in Rwanda, which took place 25 years ago, and the Cambodia genocide marks its 40th anniversary. When Holocaust victims get a chance to share and talk about their stories, it passes the responsibility to other people. All that is required of them is to respect their experience and combine efforts to ensure all Jews are safe, and no one, regardless of their ethnicity, should ever face such animosity ever again. As the world unites to remember Holocaust victims, their voices remind people of the need to work together to ensure a safe future for Europe.

Holocaust Lies and Denials

Many years later, after the Holocaust, the lies and anti-Semitism components that led to millions of deaths still spread in the world. The hatred, discrimination, and prejudice targeting Jews can still be felt. It is still alive two centuries later and regarded as lies or the truth distorted with lies.

Scientists from America and Europe classified humankind into small races, including the Semitic race.

This was where the Jews fell in, and which led to the creation of the term "anti-Semitism" by the Germans. Wilhelm Marr wrote the first piece of literature painting the Jews, entitled *The Victory of Judaism over Germandom*. It was full of nothing but lies and false myths about the Jews. He described the Jews as aliens who had the intention to destroy Germany. He founded the League Anti-Semites to fight a threat that was only in his imagination. This 1879, the political organization later gained support in the 20th-century genocide.

Anti-Semitism showed that the Germans and Jews had some intellectual and physical differences, and that they were irreversible and biologically permanent. Discrimination was justified due to this difference, and modern science played a role in it.

Even after six million Jews lost their lives, some are still in denial regarding the Holocaust. They believe that the Nazis' activities during the Second World War did not take place. There has been a long process to deny and cover up the genocide crime. It was attempted even before the war was over, and continued after and up to today.

The Holocaust left the world devastated. The mass murder and deadly gas chambers left many shocked. Since 1945, when Germany's military was defeated, there have been many attempts to whitewash and make people forget about the genocide.

The Nazi apologists did this because they have political, commercial, and ideological reasons. Some claimed to do this cover-up to help preserve the Germans' honor because the Holocaust made the German people guilty of war crimes. Nothing so horrific had ever taken place, and for patriotism's sake, other collaborators portrayed the crimes in an honorable way. They admitted that the acts were not right, but go ahead to honor those who committed them, and so they are not different from those that spread lies.

The ideological aspect is the denial state that shows how anti-Semitism is still viable in some areas of Germany and other societies across the world. The denial is expressed in various ways, including mass media, literature, art, and films. The literature is the most common tool used to express the denial of the genocide, and it is expressed in the form of pseudo-scientific research supported with some scholarly apparatus to give it credibility and show objectivity.

The academic essays full of mockery, sarcasm, and irony bring out the denial of the Holocaust. It comes from a view of some people and is based on xenophobia, nationalism, and prejudices. They are afraid that the Jews can use the facts to get political and spiritual empathy. The deniers are aware of the Holocaust and how it took place. They deny it because they support it and blame it on the Jews.

From a political view, the denial of the Holocaust seeks to bring back autocracy and fascism instead of democracy. Furthermore, they are aware that no one will ever accept dictatorship and despotism because they are associated with massive genocide.

Deniers are busy taking different forms to support anti-Semitism, and they ignore all the known cases that affected even non-Jews. It is well-known that tens of thousands of people of German origin were killed in gas chambers and in the euthanasia campaigns.

Another motivation to deny the Holocaust is for commercial purposes. Those who produce audios, videos, books, and other forms of content make a lot of money because there are people who want to believe that the Holocaust never happened. While some of the money is earned through sales, others are donations made anonymously.

How Are the Denial And Lies Spread?

Holocaust denial and lies are spread in various ways, and they include ignoring the obvious and well-known facts along with manipulating the credible sources and minimizing all the genocide dimensions in a bid to trivialize and rationalize the Holocaust by claiming how unacceptable these things are as examples of what happened during the war. These deniers lie about the major facts that define the Holocaust, and they include:

- They seek to deny that gas chambers ever existed.
- They dwell on the capacity of the cemetery camps, which are believed to be too many to have been created due to natural deaths.
- They try to reduce how enormous the crime was.

When they use the words "Polish concentration camps," these deniers are trying to make the victims look like perpetrators. This is according to Yisrael Gutman, a professor from the Yad Vashem Memorial Institute in Israel. They either do it consciously or unconsciously, but their purpose is of blurring any responsibility associated with them.

But why deny the existence of the deadly gas chambers? One is to lower the magnitude of the crime, and secondly, to prove that people have always died in such or lesser scale throughout the world's history. Besides this, the whole world was at war, and things that the Nazis did are just examples of what war can bring to humankind.

In 1973, one of the Auschwitz "witnesses" denied the existence of the gas chambers. It was transcribed and titled *Auschwitz Luge*, which means Auschwitz is a lie. This became the propaganda used to be neo-Nazi. The witness was categorical and went ahead to put to rubbish the claims of mistreatments and cruelty at the camp. It is believed that those who opposed Hitler were treated as traitors. But, this witness denied all these claims and said that what people believed to be a death camp was, in fact, a place for injured trainees to recover.

Since the late 80s, these liars and Holocaust deniers started looking for appealing and objective ways to prove the genocide is a lie. This included an analysis of chemical samples collected from the gas chambers' walls. These experts collected samples posing like tourists and later had them analyzed. Of course, they would not have a lot of hydrogen cyanide compounds that were used to kill people. This led to the conclusion that no such things took place. They use these analyses to spread lies that people were not killed in gas chambers, and that they actually never existed.

In 1988, what was dubbed as "expert analysis" was released, and was called the *Leuchter Report*. It was published by one American, and the deniers proclaimed it as an international analysis. However, it turned out that he was an execution equipment dealer. According to Leuchter's report, the amount of hydrogen cyanide found in the chamber's walls was less than what was in the disinfection chamber' walls. This led to the conclusion that it was an area used for disinfection.

The discrepancy in these reports resulted due to the fact that these chambers were used for both disinfection and killing people. The killing period was 30 minutes every day, while the rest of the time, it was used for disinfection procedures that would last between 24 and 48 hours. The chambers used for disinfection are still standing, but the gas chambers have been exposed to harsh weather, and, therefore, the hydrogen cyanide compounds would have been diluted.

What the liars and deniers seek is to raise questions regarding how the gas chambers were used to kill people or burn corpses in large numbers. Leuchter went deep to the extent of saying that a single gas chamber could not fit more than 278 people. He assumed they were all standing, assuming each occupied about one square meter. But the reality is that people were squeezed up in a small room. According to history, each room would fit in 2000 people, and they would be killed at a time. He went ahead to say that the chamber would need a week to be aired, but it was baseless and offered no evidence to support his point.

It is a well-known fact that those who removed the bodies wore masks to get rid of the bodies. When the liars say it took a week, they contradict with the instructions given by the camp administration that always reminded the SS men not to enter after the use of Zyklon B until five hours were over.

The *Leuchter Report* went ahead to question the crematorium capacity. He stated that each body is burned at a time and wondered how all the bodies got burned. In history, it is well-known that the bodies were burned in several numbers at a go. He says a single crematorium can handle not more than 715 bodies in a week, but realistically, it should burn about 315. This was one lie that the deniers found useful, and are still using to make people believe the Holocaust never happened.

Since they are lying and trying to cover the truth, their chemical analysis ends up contradicting the statements given by even the commandant in charge of Auschwitz. According to one German document talking about cremation that was compiled on the 28th of June 1943 by the Central Construction Board in Auschwitz, Birkenau and Auschwitz camps had five crematoria with the capacity to burn over 4,756 corpses within a day. It went ahead to state that the Birkenau was the most efficient crematorium, and could burn up to 1 million humans per year.

These facts bring the lies and denial in the false report by Leuchter. It has no proper understanding of the Auschwitz, and only wants to hide the truth beneath an academic-looking analysis. Anyone without any scholarly exposure will believe the calculations and graphs, and especially those who are in denial.

Germar Rudolf was a respected chemist and highly honored by Planck Institute, which later disavowed him off all his efforts in chemistry. He did this type of research between 1991 and 1992. Due to his lies and denial, he was convicted to serve a 14-month jail term. He chose to run away to England and later moved to the U.S., where they deported him to Germany in 2005. He was convicted again for lying about the existence of the deadly gas chambers. He was jailed for one and a half years.

The other report full of lies was prepared by Walter Luft in the U.S. It surfaced around 1992. He was an engineer and served in the engineering chamber of Australia as the chairman. He conducted several experiments and even appeared in courts as a witness to explain how the human body would respond in the gas chamber's temperature and how fast Zyklon B would evaporate. He concluded that the gas chamber mass killing was impossible, as the law of nature would not allow it. He also explained further that the human body couldn't be burned in batches, as it is not flammable. He was lucky to be set free by the court, which stated that he was not likely to repeat the same mistake.

In Germany, it's a crime to deny the Holocaust, and this applies to other European countries, too. This is why neo-Nazi lies and denials are taken to the U.S. or Canada. These countries are not strict about how such propaganda is spread. This gives the perpetrators all the freedom they want.

The most famous denier of the Holocaust is David Irving from the U.K. He is not a qualified historian, but has written about World War II, and in his content, he is a pro-Nazi sympathizer. He is quick to deny any Jews being killed in gas chambers, and is actually testifying in defense of Zundel. The German government has not spared him; he was fined and jailed for three years.

Misconceptions and Distortions of the Holocaust

Over time, facts about the Holocaust have been shared through generations. Even though there is a truthful source, distorted information has also been shared. The actual details have been manipulated, possibly to fit the agenda of the teller. Unfortunately, the survivors who are alive today are too aged to argue.

Distorting the Holocaust events or downplaying its horror has become common. Some people do not realize the catastrophe of World War II fully. They promote captivating information without thinking about the effects of the misconception of the Holocaust.

Fallacies are bad for the memory. The Holocaust is an event that will never go away. Information will always be available, but unfortunately, not all the stories will give the actual details. Today, you will find different versions of incidences that happened during the Holocaust. Even though these accounts are not lies, you will realize that the little details are slanted. Something else is added, and parts of the story are missing.

The Internet is a leading cause of the misconception of this tragic part of his history. The infectivity of people today has no barriers. Internet users post memes or even self-created versions of the Holocaust. This can mislead someone who does not know the facts. This leads to a debate and disagreements about the actual happenings or details of the Holocaust.

One misconception is that native Norwegians supported Jewish Norwegians by adorning paper clips. This made Norwegians sound like great and humane people, as the story is told. However, the truth behind the paper clip was used by the Norwegian citizens to show their support for their King, Haakon VII. It was insignificant to the Holocaust, and distorting it to look like it was a cause for World War II is misleading. Though Norwegians wore the paper clips, it is crucial to avoid the fallacy that alludes to the meaning of the paper clip use.

Another distortion of the Holocaust is the use of crushed bone to construct the Autobahn. It is said that the Germans crushed the bones of the victims and used to develop the highway system. This does not add up, because the events supposedly happened in 1942, but the systems were built much later in the 50s, after the death of Hitler. Looking at the provisions of the historical facts, the Germans crushed the bones of the victims buried in mass graves to get rid of the evidence of the mass killings.

Rumor on Hitler's Lineage

There are some misconceptions about the population growth of the Jewish people in Germany. Even though there was a high number of Jews who lived in Germany, the facts are biased. Jews made up less than 2% of the German population, even then. The highest number of Jews lived in Poland, making them nearly 10% of the population. Another claim is about Adolf Hitler's Jewish origin. It is rumored that Hitler's father may have been a son of the Jew that Hitler's grandmother worked for. Historically, this has not been proven. It has given ways to other misconceptions, such as Hitler's hidden health history.

The Jewish Doctor

There is a misconception on what may have triggered Hitler's hatred toward Jews. Some people say that when Hitler's mother fell ill, a Jewish doctor who treated Klara Hitler may have failed to offer the right diagnosis or treatment, leading to the woman's death. Historians have found evidence that this may be a misconception. The doctor testified that Hitler did not harbor any hard feelings. He gave a testimony in the United States in 1943. Hitler protected the doctor and allowed him to leave with his family. These ruled out any hatred Hitler may have had toward him.

Soap Made from Jewish Bodies

Human hair or dental gold was removed from the Jewish bodies and sold. Evidence has been found in plenty to support these facts. However, the use of Jewish bodies to make soap is a misconception. There is no evidence to prove this. Pieces of old soap taken from the concentration camps have to be analyzed to check for human DNA, and none has been found.

The information distorts the facts; Jewish corpses were either burned or buried. Historians have found that Heinrich Himmler sent a strict directive to the head of Gestapo to make sure that no such thing was taking place. He wanted a confirmation report that there was no soap production using the Jewish corpses. He further ordered that the bodies be disposed of by burning or burying them.

Denmark Star Badge

In Denmark, it is misconstrued that King Christian X wore a star budge to support his Jewish citizens. It is correct to say that the king supported the Jewish population in Denmark and declined to support the Nazi ideology, but he did not adorn the star badge. The king remained supportive of his population and encouraged peaceful coexistence by taking an unescorted ride around the city.

The Jewish Controlled Foreign Economies

Jews made the elite class of German ruling and business class for many years; this is a distortion of the truth. In Europe, Jews were vilified for being non-Christians. They did not control the economy from an elitist point of view; they were viewed as cons who took advantage of others to make money. They were seen as heartless and money-driven.

This is the perception that Hitler is said to have twisted and used to convince others that Jews wanted to take over the world. This was further distorted by classifying Jews as a race, even though they were a religious group made of different ethnic groups. They were targeted with a view that the race could be totally annihilated from the world. Germans failed to understand that religion goes beyond race.

Adolf Hitler's Death

Misconceptions surround the life of Adolf Hitler. Some people say that he is still alive because a proxy was killed, and he made an escape. This is misleading. Furthermore, the cause of his death is still debated. Some say he shot himself, while others insist that he ingested poison. History has proved that he died in a hiding place after ingesting cyanide, shot himself, and the body set ablaze by his supporters.

Other Forms of Denial and Distortion of the Truth

The Holocaust is actually among the correctly documented events, which occurred years ago and is regarded as a bad history. Normally, its denial and distortion are motivated by the hatred of Jews. Besides that, it is founded on claims that it was invented by the Jews in order to address their own interests and needs.

As such, people's ability to deny the events of the said Holocaust is an attempt to negate Nazi genocide facts. The main assertion of its denial is that killings of about six million Jews did not happen during World War II, and this includes hiding the truth that poison gas chambers did not exist, and the Nazis did not have any official policy to eliminate the Jews. The latest trend is the distortion of all truths about the Holocaust facts.

The most common ones include assertions that about 5 million people who were murdered seems to be an exaggeration. Additionally, deaths that happened in concentration camps were caused by starvation or ailments, but not policy. Also, another assertion is that Anne Frank's diary is just forgery.

Just like any other propaganda and rumors, the distortion, misuse, and denial of the Holocaust are just strategies to meet the following goals:

- To attract attention to certain issues.
- To compromise Israel's legitimacy. In fact, some believe that it was established to compensate all the Jews who suffered during the Holocaust.
- To decrease the sympathy directed toward the Jews.
- To bring about doubts on the Holocaust and the Jews.

The Legality of Denying the Holocaust

The United States constitution promotes and assures freedom of speech. Because of this, engaging in hate speech or even denying the Holocaust is your right, since you have freedom of speech and expression. However, you are not allowed to use hate speech whenever there is a threat of violence or property damage.

Unlike in the U.S., most European countries where the killing of Jews occurred have set laws criminalizing hate speech, as well as denial of the Holocaust. The above two different legal frameworks hinder a reputable and sophisticated approach to contest the denial of the Holocaust.

The denial and distortion of facts are encouraged by agendas that are neither related to the comprehension of historical events, nor about the Holocaust. Some people, commonly referred to as the "deniers of the Holocaust", claim that they are scholars, but they just manipulated ideas, which simply support certain ideological positions. In addition, they just claim to provide a different version of its history to hide their intentions under the guise of free speech.

To find out whether a claim falls between a spectrum of its denial as well as distortion, you are recommended to consider the following facts:

- What is the intention of the source? Is it to make you believe after exposing you to the information?
- Is the source reliable, or has it provided historical exaggerations?
- Are the facts being presented by your source supportive of the claim?
- Does the source bring out a certain belief or idea?
- Does the source adhere to a particular set of methods to inquire about historical claims and events?
- Is the claim presented in the source really fitting within the generally accepted Holocaust history?

It is clear that the case of the deformation of the Holocaust possesses numerous questions. The book, *The Abuse of Holocaust Memory*, provides statements, incidents, and a phenomenon divided into eight major categories. However, a few years back, the number of events has increased. Now, it may be impossible to overlook the whole region if systematic monitoring is not put in position by an institution. Also, another aspect is that the manipulation of the truth about the Holocaust may turn out to be a debate.

Reasons That the Holocaust Will Not Fade Away

Why is the attention given to the Holocaust increasing? This is generally because it is the nature of historical events.

Although you can't quantify the entire situation, qualitative indications of Holocaust abuse are often increasing. This is because, when you start researching it, you take note of how diverse it is.

Whenever you commence looking for a reason, some causes emerge. They include the following:

- A trend which can lead to an increase in chaos and violence in the world.
- Increment of barrier removal to what is allowed and acceptable in public domain or particular places.
- One of the greatest sources of Holocaust distortion increment is social media, since it is not regulated.

Denial of the Holocaust is a rejection of core facts regarding the elimination of the people of the Jewish community during World War II. After David Irving lost his case in court in the year 2000 against Penguin Publishers, as well as Deborah Lipstadt, there was hope that the denial of the Holocaust would fade away. Iran has been the major reviver of the Holocaust. However, in Western countries, its denial seems to be rising slowly. This is concluded after focusing on a report by David Collier, who is a British researcher, and who focuses on social media.

In the report, it is found that, in social media platforms like Facebook, SPSC compares Nazi Germany to Israel, anti-Semitic slurs, and Holocaust denial. The people who are not ready to accept historical events are the common victims of distorted opinion about the Holocaust. They do not want to accept the crimes committed during the Nazi era. They know the truth, but choose to deny the Holocaust. Other people who believe lies are those who know nothing about history. They accept the views of the revisionists spread by propagandists.

Polish Holocaust Revisionism

Currently, there are multiple new disclosures on some of the actual crimes that were committed against the people of the Jewish community. Two scholars, Jan Gross and Jan Grabowski, have focused majorly on this subject. All attention is, therefore, channeled to the individuals who denied the events of the Holocaust.

Conclusion

The painful truth of the Holocaust survivors is once again with us as we mark its hurtful anniversary. It is my greatest hope that you have gone through the entire book, amid sobs, and thirst to quench your love for the historical work. This book, *Surviving the Holocaust,* takes us to the atrocities that occurred during the World War II genocide.

The main aim of this book is to help us understand all the circumstances that led to the massive killings of the Jews living in Germany, and its collaborators. It is hurtful to note that over six million people lost their dear lives, with another eleven million feared to be unaccounted for. The book also talks about survivors who told their genocide stories, and how they managed to evade the satanic sword of death.

It would be unfair if we fail to mention survivors of the Holocaust, such as Irene Fogel Weiss, Joseph Salomonovic, David Mermelstein, and many others. For you to fully understand this, I urge you to pay more attention to the chapters describing their lives, as these are put in detail.

Another objective of this book is to help you with enough knowledge that you would want to know about the perpetrators of the genocide. It is my pleasure that you will concentrate on the areas touching the likes of Adolf Hitler and the rest.

Surviving the Holocaust initiates you into a world of a painful slur. It is better to note that many people lost their lives, and over sixty million people could not find a home to settle into completely.

Even though the Germans and their collaborators went ahead to justify their genocide, which took place between 1941 and 1945, no one will ever accept the ruthless killings of over seventeen million people. It is going to be a permanent scar that lives on with each generation. It is with much regret that, even after the releasing of some prisoners, these survivors could not go back to their homes. Their mind is completely against this, as they call their homeland a "cursed land". Therefore, it would be better if you take your time and concentrate on these chapters, elaborating much about the survivors' decisions. Can you think of a situation where a prisoner is set free but fails to go back to his or her homeland?

Surviving the Holocaust also takes us to the world of lies, denials, perceptions, and much more. It is my pleasure that you can take your time to go through all these chapters to talk about the lies, the way denials have escalated, and how everyone thinks that all these are just perceptions.

The book goes further ahead to introduce a tone of forgiveness, even though many Jews still think that this is not over. The hatred still lingers in their minds, even after many social organizations have come up with different reconciliation ways.

It is my hope that the book was helpful, and that you look forward to engaging the masses with a view of creating peace amongst you. It is also my hope that you will be in a position to stand firm against any ruthless ruling employed by any leader in future.

Korman's Prayer

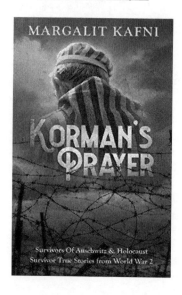

To live through the atrocities of World War II and the worst work camp in history, will no doubt change a person.

It shows how despite the worst circumstances, people can still show love and compassion toward one another. It strives to show that no matter how cruel the torture, the one thing the enemy cannot take is our spirit.

This novel is inspired by the story of Henry Korman's life. It will give you an in-depth look at what life was like inside the barbed-wire fences of Auschwitz. It will also show you the effect that these experiences had on one man, leading him away from anger and hate, toward a life of service to others. A few years before he died, Henry was quoted as saying: "I worry what will happen when I and others like me are no longer here to tell the story. I want people to keep reading about it and for them to leave tears on the paper."

I hope that this book does exactly that.

Margalit Kafni

READ NOW ON AMAZON

Made in the USA
Columbia, SC
15 August 2021